MOONLIGHT AT THE GLOBE

MOONLIGHT
AT THE GLOBE

An Essay in Shakespeare Production
based on performance of *A Midsummer Night's Dream*
at Harrow School

by

RONALD WATKINS

drawings by
MAURICE PERCIVAL

★

FOREWORD BY
R. W. MOORE
(*Head Master of Harrow*)

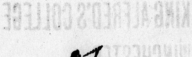

MICHAEL JOSEPH LTD.
26 *Bloomsbury Street, London,* W.C.1

FIRST PUBLISHED 1946

★

To

MY MOTHER

★

*Set and printed in Great Britain by Tonbridge
Printers Ltd., Peach Hall Works, Tonbridge,
in Baskerville eleven on twelve point, and
bound by James Burn*

*"but there is two hard things: that is, to
bring the Moone-light into a chamber . . ."*

In quotation from the play, the spelling of the Fisher Quarto of 1600—except in obvious cases of misprint—has been preserved. This was the only form in which Shakespeare himself can have read his play in print.

The line-reference is that of MacMillan's *Globe Edition*.

Foreword

"ALL EVENTS," a wise man has said, "have causes, and most events have many causes." If we may consider our present mode of Shakespeare production at Harrow as an event, its causes may be diagnosed with an almost Aristotelian precision. There is the fact of our contemporaneity as a school with the "Avon's child"; do we not sing in one of our songs

> *For we began when he began,*
> *Our times are one;*
> *His glory thus shall circle us*
> *Till time be done?*

The inference, though it is born not of arrogance but of piety, may be unduly optimistic; but the premiss is founded on fact. There is the formal cause that in Speech Room, with its semi-circular auditorium, its spacious well and its easy acoustic properties, we possess as promising a ready-made theatre as could be desired for a mimic Globe. There is the efficient cause in the German fire-bomb whose contribution is described on a later page. There is a material cause in the scholarship of Mr. John Cranford Adams, the publication of whose volume on the Globe Playhouse was greeted at Harrow as an epoch-making event; thanks to him we now know what the Globe theatre was really like. And there is, as *causa causans*, combining and pointing all these factors, the creative insight and infectious virtuosity of Mr. Ronald Watkins.

Few who saw his productions of *Twelfth Night*, *Henry V* and *Macbeth* will forget them, but his production of *A Mid-*

summer Night's Dream surpassed them all. We knew then
that, despite all the tricks of the modern stage, there was
only one way of playing Shakespeare. As we warmed our
hands over the fire with Theseus and Hippolyta, we felt that
Nick Bottom and Peter Quince were our henchmen and
familiars and, when the comely couples had ascended to
their bedchambers and somewhere down West Street
Bottom and his friends were already snoring, we knew that
Titania had really come to the Hill and, in her incarnate,
the faery soul of Arden, domiciled as safely as the lovers
when the tapers had flitted their benedictory round, and
never to be affrighted from our citadel till some blundering
hand should resurrect the clogging curtain and the banal
floodlight.

Yes, it is indeed the only way; to give the actors just such
scope as they had at the Globe and to let the poetry work its
magic for itself: and I hope that this little book will serve to
convince many others that it is the only way. That this book
is a labour of love need hardly be said; it is more than that.
It is a testimony to a corporate effort which was an inspiration to those who shared it and to those who witnessed, and
a notable contribution to Shakespearian scholarship and to
the craft of the theatre. Also, we hope, it is only a beginning.

R. W. MOORE

Harrow, 1946.

Preface

He who to-day writes on a Shakespearian theme must inevitably owe more to his predecessors than he can easily acknowledge or indeed himself be fully aware of. Through the work of critics of such varying approach as Sir Edmund Chambers, Dr. W. W. Greg, Dr. J. Semple Smart, Professor J. Dover Wilson and Dr. E. M. W. Tillyard, and the body of opinion collected by Dr. H. Granville-Barker and Dr. G. B. Harrison in the *Cambridge Companion to Shakespeare Studies*, it is now possible, in spite of discrepancies and disagreements, to recognize an orthodox creed in Shakespearian scholarship. To this orthodoxy I gladly subscribe and count myself as others fortunate in having such clear guidance on a road where it is only too easy to lose one's way.

The present essay on *A Midsummer Night's Dream* attempts to interpret the play from the viewpoint of the Chamberlain's Men and outlines a modern production on the pattern of a supposed performance at the Globe: it is therefore largely speculative, often trying for the sake of completeness to find a practical solution where exact scholarship would prefer to suspend judgment. It is especially indebted to the collected *Prefaces* of Dr. Granville-Barker (though it was not till after my book was in the press that I had the opportunity of comparing conclusions with his preface to this particular play, published by Ernest Benn Limited, in the *Players' Shakespeare*). Dr. Granville-Barker's recent death removes from the field of Shakespearian criticism the most eloquent champion of Shakespeare's stagecraft. I owe much also to Mr. J. Cranford Adams's recent study of *The Globe Playhouse*;

A*

to the *New Cambridge Shakespeare* edition of the play, with the characteristic contributions of Sir Arthur Quiller-Couch and Professor Dover Wilson; and for discussion of the music, to Mr. Richmond Noble's *Shakespeare's Use of Song*.

A more personal word of thanks is due to many friends at Harrow; to Mr. R. W. Moore, the Head Master, without whose encouragement and help this book would not have been written; to Mr. Maurice Percival, whose drawings illustrate these pages, for his patient and stimulating collaboration both in the production of the play at Harrow and in the shaping of the book; to Mr. Hector McCurrach, who provided the Elizabethan musical score of which an account is given below, and to Mr. Geoffrey Mendham, who directed its performance; and to all those who were concerned, whether on or off the stage of Speech Room, with the performance of *A Midsummer Night's Dream* in July, 1945, and with the four previous experiments of the series.

Finally, I am glad to have the opportunity of thanking Mr. E. V. C. Plumptre, who throughout our five-year plan of Shakespeare at Harrow has stood at the producer's elbow with helpful criticism and advice; and Mr. J. W. Moir who has read the proofs of this book with patient care and made many valuable suggestions on points of detail.

R. W.

CONTENTS

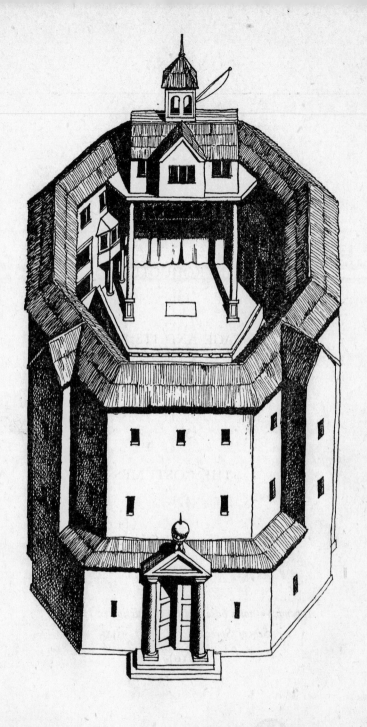

I

INTRODUCTION

*

SHAKESPEARE was not only a great poet; he was also a great dramatist—indeed, it would be difficult to find in any other playwright a greater mastery of the art of the theatre. The point needs stressing. Moreover, there is no reason to doubt that this particular art was his deliberate choice as a means of expression, that he was possessed by a passion for the drama, conceived perhaps some day when he stood gazing with the eye of childhood in fearful delight upon the travelling mummers on their visit to Stratford. We know that for more than ten years, in the course of which most of his finest plays were written, he was an active member of the most successful company of players in London, and assisted in the production of his plays, which were the chief cause of that success. Yet since the disappearance of the unlocalized stage, the stage of undefined scene, for which he wrote, and of the conditions and conventions of his playhouse, his countrymen, for all their admiration, have been slow to acknowledge the peculiar nature of his dual genius. Renowned critics have declared his plays unfitted for the theatre: devotees of unquestioned culture prefer to worship their idol by the fireside: and even the pundits of his own profession still, as in the days of Garrick, give in effect the same verdict by letting it be thought that something must be done beyond what Shakespeare himself did to make the plays palatable to a modern audience. So we have every kind of experiment of lighting and scenery and costume, we see Shakespeare in modern dress and in technicolour, we have irrelevant spectacle and irrelevant "business," passages are left out on the ground that Shakespeare did not know what was "good theatre," and sometimes speeches are inserted from other plays, to repair their author's oversight.

But when all is said, there is only one thing that needs doing. If it is believed that Shakespeare well knew what he was about and indeed had genius in his particular art, then plainly the producer's first task is to discover in what that genius lay, to study the medium in which Shakespeare was working, and to recapture the essential conditions of his theatre. The practical difficulty of this task is not great, but it needs a preliminary act of faith. William Poel and Harley Granville-Barker, inspired with that faith, have written eloquently to urge the claims of Shakespeare's own stage, and have been boldly venturous in putting their belief to the test of performance. But few in this generation are old enough to have had the chance of seeing Poel's Elizabethan productions,[1] and perhaps even by him the experiment was never made with full acceptance of all the implications of his belief. It means, for instance, that we must risk launching a boy-actor in broad daylight into the middle of his audience, and bid him with no more aid than a flickering candle persuade them that he is a murderess walking in her sleep; no more aid—except Shakespeare's words. Such an attempt challenges the imagination of actor and audience alike to a communal suspension of disbelief, and faith has its reward, if the challenge is taken up on both sides.

It means also that we must pay more attention and respect to that company of players who worked with Shakespeare to create the plays when they first appeared on the stage. Here is a field of enquiry which has hitherto not been thoroughly explored: the way to begin is to consider each play afresh from their point of view, to ask how they would have tackled

---

[1] A list of performances of the Elizabethan Stage Society can be found in William Poel's *Shakespeare in the Theatre* (Sidgwick & Jackson, 1913), pp. 206ff.; and some account of his and Granville-Barker's productions, together with mention of other experiments in the same vein, is given in Harold Child's chapter in the *Cambridge Companion to Shakespeare Studies*, pp. 345-6.

it, to reconstruct the problems which confronted them and attempt to solve them as they would have done. There has been a popular tendency to belittle or at least ignore the Chamberlain's Men, as if they were a body of crude and incompetent barn-stormers, working in primitive conditions.[1] Granville-Barker has been at pains to dispel this illusion, and has pointed the way to a return to the Elizabethan playhouse; but, being himself a practising artist in the modern theatre, with its hampering conditions always at his elbow, he has not been able to push his beliefs to their logical conclusion. We have still to see in England a reconstruction of the original Globe, with the right partition of stage and auditorium and the right tradition of performance to create the atmosphere in which alone Shakespeare's poetry can have its full dramatic force.

In the following pages an attempt is made to reconsider an early play which, though it does not need all the resources of the Globe, yet gains greatly from being set in its proper perspective; and to fit it, with the aid of the Chamberlain's Men, to the essential conditions of Shakespeare's theatre— the intimate size of the auditorium, the vast proportions of the platform, the steady daylight, the inset "study" at the back, and the available resources of personnel and music and costume and properties. *A Midsummer Night's Dream* is not strictly a Globe play at all. It is generally agreed that in its original form it was designed for a court wedding, and it was probably revised more than once for other likewise private occasions. But the title-page of the Fisher Quarto,[2] the basis of our present text of the play, suggests a number of public performances, and Dover Wilson, in the course of his note on "The Copy for *A Midsummer Night's Dream*, 1600," argues that it was in the repertory of the Chamberlain's Men between 1598 and 1600.[3] If this is so, the play

---

[1] The tendency persists in spite of the evidence supplied by indefatigable research, such as that of Professor T. W. Baldwin in his *The Organization and Personnel of the Shakespearean Company* (Princeton, 1927).

[2] Reproduced below, p. 108.

[3] M.N.D. (*New Cambridge Shakespeare*), p. 97.

was adapted at this time—presumably by Shakespeare himself, certainly with his connivance—for use on the public stage, and we may suppose that it was one of the plays done on the stage of the Globe in the first year of its existence.

Such a performance in 1599 is the model of what follows. In considering its probable shape, it is extraordinary how much can be deduced or inferred from the text of the play itself: the dramatist's instructions are embedded in the words of the speakers. Indeed, it seems as if this is part of the secret of poetic drama. Few even of the original stage-directions in the canon add to our understanding of characters or situations; but often enough the words of the text will tell us not only what the characters are like or what the scene is supposed to be, but also how we ought to feel about the people or what impression the circumstances should be making on our minds. Cæsar's vivid character-sketch of that spare Cassius is a clear indication to the actor how to play the part; it is also calculated to make us in the audience afraid of the conspirator with the lean and hungry look. On the night before Agincourt, we not only watch the poor condemned English sitting round their camp-fires; we are made keenly sensible of their dejection and the relief of Harry's presence—the little touch of Harry in the night. We not only see the darkness falling on the night of Banquo's death, but we are filled with a panic desire to escape from it: we, too, spur apace with the lated traveller to gain the timely inn. We feel its evil influence irresistibly in Macbeth's terrible invocation—"Come, feeling Night, ſkarfe vp the tender Eye of pittifull Day." Our own tender and pitiful sensibilities, too, are oppressed with the weight of Macbeth's murderous mood. By many such strokes of Shakespeare's genius, the stark conditions of his theatre are turned to opportunity. This is the true poetic drama, and not merely a play with dialogue in verse. So likewise with *A Midsummer Night's Dream* more often than not Shakespeare's instructions to actors and audience are contained in the words. Sometimes, of course, in the suggested setting that follows, guesswork has been necessary, but the guesses are based on probability in the light of what we know of the period, of the acting companies, of the music of the day, and above all of the tastes and opinions of Shakespeare himself, as expressed for instance in the celebrated passages of *Hamlet* on the theatre.

The play has suffered much from those who would add another hue unto the rainbow. The first need has been to get rid of all such excess—whether of scenery, of costume, or of music. It is like removing the over-painting from a "restored" masterpiece. The reward, if the process is successful, is to contemplate for the first time the masterpiece as the painter painted it. If the costume and music here suggested in place of the habitual decorations risk incurring the charge of being still not Shakespeare, excuse must be sought in the reflection that a play does not come to its full life until it is presented on the stage, that for this purpose costume and music are needed, and that to this extent the dramatist must always have been indebted to the collaboration of others for the realisation of his purpose. It is thought that the collaboration sketched below would not only have been available in Shakespeare's theatre, but have had the approval of Shakespeare himself.[1]

It is hoped that this attempted restoration of one play of Shakespeare's to the conditions of his own theatre will help to prove the contention that this is the only way to taste the full flavour of his poetic drama, and that by a similar approach other plays in the canon, too, would be seen as their creator intended them. Shakespeare, it is here asserted, knew what he was about all the time; his stagecraft is masterly; he was an actor as well as a poet, and he knew the secret of poetic drama. A task still waiting the attention of Shakespearian scholars is to re-examine all the plays through

---

[1] This reconstruction of the play has been tested in performance. *A Midsummer Night's Dream* was produced on these lines in Harrow School Speech Room in July, 1945—the fourth of a series of experiments in the Elizabethan production of Shakespeare, which began in 1941. Some account of this performance, with details of the stage-arrangements and the musical score, is given in the Appendix.

the eyes of the Chamberlain's Men, confronted with the
practical problem of staging them for the first time at the
Globe, the Blackfriars, or elsewhere. Until this examination
is made, and the results translated from theory into practice,
the real nature of Shakespeare's poetic drama will remain
concealed. It is a strange thought that still, after more than
three hundred years of general acclamation, we have never
seen the full splendour of the art we are so ready to admire.

2

THE STAGE AND ITS SETTINGS

*

JOHN CRANFORD ADAMS's study of the Globe Playhouse,[1] with its detailed scale-drawings, makes an exact reconstruction for the first time a practical possibility; and it corrects at once the notion that the theatre was a primitive make-shift. The Globe emerges from his book rather as a most expressive and pliant instrument for the exhibition of the dramatist's art, evolved from primitive practice, but developed and planned by the experience and from the needs of a syndicate of seven professionals of the theatre, of which Shakespeare and Burbage were members. There is a

---

[1] John Cranford Adams, *The Globe Playhouse, Its Design and Equipment* (Harvard University Press, 1943).

corollary, that the company who devised this playhouse for their own use knew well what they were about and were satisfied with their medium. We must not take too seriously the elaborate apologies that heralded the opening perform-

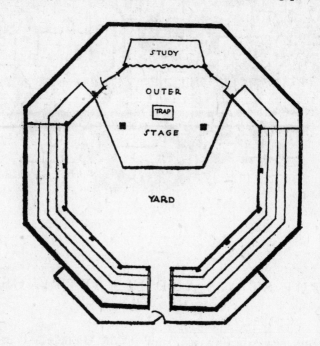

ances at "this Woodden O". They are of a piece with the almost automatic self-depreciation of Shakespeare's refer-ences to his profession of player. The theatre was his chosen art, and he revelled in it for twenty years. The Globe was, for at least ten, the vehicle of that art, and the Globe was not merely of his choice, but, we may almost say, of his building.

Most striking in Cranford Adams's drawings are the pro-portions of the stage itself. No mere "apron" will do, jutting out as an extra-territorial annexe to the picture-stage behind the proscenium. The platform projects to the very centre of the building, the middle of its front edge being the central point of the whole frame, a regular octagon. A glance at Cranford Adams's diagram of the ground plan suggests that there is an artistic rightness about this proportion.[1] Its effect is compelling, and transforms our notions of the drama. The vast field of action is surrounded on three sides by the audience: movement on the stage is in the midst of the assembled company, and affects them with a direct contact; the solitary Hamlet will here speak intimately to the heart of each individual hearer, but Mark Antony will sway the whole audience as well as his stage-crowd with the frenzy of mob-emotion: armies confronting each other in this arena will seem to split the house into hostile camps; the spectators make a ring for a swordsmen's duel; the ears of the groundlings will often be in danger of splitting. At the back of this great platform stands the tiring-house, with its complicated structure built on three levels, and six distinct stages for the use of the resourceful dramatist.[2] To restore such plays as *Hamlet* and *Antony and Cleopatra* and *The Tempest* to the setting of this theatre for which they were devised would undoubtedly shed new light on their stagecraft and give a much clearer impression of each play than has been seen since the days of Shakespeare himself.

IT would be a matter of much interest to make such a restoration, even on paper; still more to see it done in a new Globe Playhouse, rebuilt with all the intricate structure and equipment of the original. Meanwhile *A Midsummer Night's Dream* would not have employed the full resources of the theatre: it may even be that this was one of

---

[1] The diagram shown is a simplification based on the plan worked out by Cranford Adams, *The Globe Playhouse*, p. 53.

[2] See below, p. 35.

√ the reasons why it was dropped from the repertory in 1600 and came into the hands of the printer. There seems no opportunity, except for a brief moment at the very end of the play, for using the second-level stages; all else will be done on ground-level.

It would be difficult to preserve the illusion of the wood on the bare scaffold-boards of the stage, and it seems likely that for this occasion—even if it was not usually done—they would be covered with a copious strewing of rushes.[1] No doubt it was found necessary, as each night-wanderer stumbled through the wood, to drown

> the woodden Dialogue and found
> 'Twixt his ftretcht footing, and the Scaffolage.

This vegetable presence would carry into the playhouse the breath of the forest, and it would serve besides for the court interior: for the custom was in the houses of the great to strew rushes on the floor.

We have then the vast platform of the fore-stage with a capacious central trap-door, and the inset "study" that can be concealed from view by curtains. The two tall pillars supporting the "heavens" will be trees in the forest or pillars in the palace at will. With these *data*, the settings emerge almost inevitably from a close study of the text. Two critical moments suggest themselves at once—the change from I. ii to II. i, where in the twinkling of an eye we must pass from a carpenter's shop to a moonlit wood; and the transition from II. i to II. ii, where at one moment Oberon speaks of the bank on which Titania habitually rests, and at the next we see her sung to sleep upon that very bank.

There is no other means of engineering the second of these two transitions than to reveal Titania's bank already in position in the inset at that moment. It follows that the

---

[1] But Cranford Adams, *The Globe Playhouse*, p. 106, infers from the opening of III. i. that the rushes were strewn only on the rear half of the outer stage.

previous scene was played on the main stage with the inset-curtain closed; and it seems very likely that the Chamberlain's Men found it convenient to reserve the first opening of the inset till this point; so that Titania's bank and Bottom's hawthorn brake could both be set in position ready before the play started.

What then did they do to carry their audience into the wood at the beginning of II. i? How in broad daylight, with no protecting proscenium curtain, did the boy-actors in 1599 suddenly persuade their audience that they were in a moonlit wood? Some simple trick of make-believe is needed such as would have appealed to Shakespeare himself—the poet who persuaded blind Gloucester on level ground that he had fallen down the precipice of Dover cliff.

The mechanicals meet, it is reasonable to suppose, in Quince's shop. Quince is a carpenter, and it is easy to shift from palace to shop if the company assemble round a carpenter's bench. Such a bench—a substantial burden, that

will strain the muscles of hard-handed men—they carry in
with them, and set down-stage of the trap-door; and round
it, sitting on stools or on the bench itself, they hold their
production committee meeting under Quince's presidency.
On the top of the bench are folded two green tarpaulins, and

their unobtrusive presence is made more plausible by
Starveling the tailor, who takes his scissors and needle to a
hem of one of them.

Towards the end of the scene—the opportunity comes
while Quince and Bottom are discussing what beard
Pyramus should wear—the rest of the craftsmen unfold the
tarpaulins and rig them over the bench and the stools in a
semi-circle masking the trap. An old tree-stump, explicable
as a carpenter's block and during the early part of the scene
used as a seat by Starveling, is placed on top of the tarpaulin,

and the company retire leaving the audience a puzzle to interpret.

Meanwhile, of course, Shakespeare has been at work long ago:

> . . . to morrow night:
> And in the wood, a league without the towne . . .

> To morrow night, when Phoebe doth beholde
> Her filuer vifage, in the watry glaffe,
> Decking, with liquid pearle, the bladed graffe . . .

> And in the wood, where often you an I,
> Vpon faint Primrofe beddes, were wont to lye . . .

> . . . till morrow deepe midnight . . .

> Then, to the wodde, will he, to morrow night,
> Purfue her . . .

These are the tongues of lovers, but the handicraftmen too are to rehearse "to morrow night", and "in the palace wood, a mile without the towne, by Moone-light . . . At the Dukes oke wee meete." The dullest groundling would begin to take the hint.

The music suggests a change of mood: in comes a Fairy, lady-in-waiting of Titania's train. What does she do? Why, decks the great green bank with flowers. How do we know that this is her occupation? She (or Shakespeare) will tell us so in a minute:

> And I ferue the Fairy Queene,
> To dew her orbs vpon the greene.
> The cowflippes tall her Penfioners bee . . .

> I muft goe feeke fome dew droppes here,
> And hang a pearle in euery couflippes eare.

She is interrupted at her task by Puck who springs out of the earth; he has been waiting for his cue under the trap-door, now hidden behind a flower-clad bank—which was once a carpenter's bench. Puck's entry from nowhere is a trick that any conjuror can play; but the creation of a wood out of

nothing needs Shakespeare's help. And by the way, it is a wood by moonlight:

> I do wander euery where;
> ſwifter than the Moons ſphere . . .

As she says it, the little Fairy's finger traces the great circle of the moon, and her eye, in a fine frenzy, watches Phœbe bowling along in her chariot through the clouds of a night sky.[1] We are ready for the entry of the King and Queen—

---

[1] The moon has been constantly kept in the front of our consciousness, from the opening speeches of the Duke and Hippolyta: Egeus speaks of Lysander's moonlight serenades, Theseus of the nun "chaunting faint hymnes, to the colde fruitleſſe Moone," the lovers' tryst is by moonlight. If whenever the moon is mentioned, the actors look up at a pre-determined quarter of the sky, the moon's presence will be irresistibly established by the time we reach the wood.

more than ready, for Puck leads us to the brink of expectation:

> And now, they neuer meete in groue, or greene,
> By fountaine cleare, or fpangled ftarlight fheene,
> But they doe fquare, that all their Elues, for feare,
> Creepe into acorne cups, and hide them there.

When the stage fills with the rival trains of Oberon and Titania, about to square, the illusion is already complete. The equipment is still no more than a rush-strewn platform, a carpenter's bench covered in tarpaulin, a tree-stump and some flowers. Shakespeare's words have turned this furniture into a moonlit wood: they were devised for just such a purpose, to transform such simple properties; and if we make no attempt to supplement the properties of Shakespeare's theatre, the words will come into their own. The words contain the secret of Shakespeare's stagecraft. If search is made, it will be found.

AT Titania's second entrance the inset-curtain is pulled for the first time. What does it disclose? The answer is unmistakably given by Shakespeare. First, there must be Titania's bank—which we have just this moment heard described by Oberon. His speech has become a "set piece"—it is even sometimes sung—and the irony of set pieces is that the words are known to be so beautiful that we forget to listen to them, to take in their sense. This is what Oberon says:

> I know a banke where the wilde time blowes,
> Where Oxlips, and the nodding Violet growes,
> Quite ouercanopi'd with lufhious woodbine,
> With fweete mufke rofes, and with Eglantine:
> There fleepes Tytania, fometime of the night,
> Luld in thefe flowers, with daunces and delight:
> And there the Snake throwes her enammeld fkinne,
> Weed wide enough to wrappe a Fairy in.

Shakespeare's audience, I take it, accustomed to the
method of his theatre, would carry the sense of this passage
in their heads for the ten lines that follow; and immediately,
as the curtain was pulled, would identify the Queen's couch,
and decorate it in imagination with the features of Oberon's
description. It would not be necessary to send forth the
property-man to buy every item of the list: the essentials are
something green for Titania to sleep on, and some overhanging leaves as a suggestion of "canopy": Oberon has
already done the rest.

It is important to recognize that this anticipatory description is a deliberate and essential stroke of Shakespeare's
stagecraft. It is not a decorative lyric nor an operatic *aria*;
its purpose is to challenge through the power of words—the
chief medium of the poetic dramatist—the imagination of
the audience to see more than their eyes can see, to accept
this pile of mattresses covered with green tapestries and
canopied with an overhanging leafy branch as the appropriate fourposter for a fairy queen.

Besides Titania's couch, Shakespeare has prescribed
another piece of stage furniture to be disclosed in the inset.
By the time the mechanicals reach their meeting-place in
the wood, they—or their creator—have forgotten the Duke's
oak. Instead, Peter Quince selects for their stage "this
greene plot"—the rushes on the fore-stage—and "this
hauthorne brake" for their tiring-house. Pyramus is instructed "when you have ſpoken your ſpeech, enter into
that Brake," and from this he emerges with the ass's nole
fixed on his head. This then is the furniture of the inset at
the Globe: on one side Titania's bank, on the other Bottom's
hawthorn-brake.

O NCE the full depth of the stage is disclosed, there is no
reason to draw the curtain again until we leave the
wood—no intrinsically dramatic reason. There is no
certainty about the practice of the Chamberlain's Men with

regard to intervals, but on the Globe stage the sleeping of the
fog-bound lovers need not hinder an interruption of the
action at the end of Act Three. They find their cold bed in
the inset—a pair on the bank, a pair beneath the brake—and
so with the pull of the curtain are given a rest from sleeping
in the public eye. Dramatically there is no need for a pause:
Shakespeare's stage-craft makes no allowance for one, and
puts no reliance on it: even before Puck covers the starry
welkin with drooping fog, he has nervously sniffed the air of
morning and seen Aurora's harbinger in the sky. "Make no
delay," says Oberon, "we may effect this bufineſſe yet ere
day." The will-o'-the-wisp sequence goes at breathless speed:
then the tempo slows for Titania's dotage: when Oberon
and Titania are reconciled, Bottom—minus the ass-head—is
left sleeping in front of the fore-stage bank. Suddenly Puck
sounds a warning—

> Fairy King, attend, and marke:
> I do heare the morning Larke.

The King and Queen, in silence sad, trip after night's shade;
and Puck, startled by the huntsman's horn, plunges into his
hole in the ground. When the stage fills with the Duke's
hunting-party, who will be in doubt that another day has
dawned?

WE cannot dispense with the wood before Bottom is
awake, has said his say and gone trotting off to
Athens. Then we must get rid of it in a hurry. The
curtain cuts us off from Titania's bower and Bottom's
hawthorn-brake. But there is still this great green bank on
the fore-stage to dispose of. Another conjuring trick is
needed; this time a very simple one. Starveling the tailor

appears, scratches his head as if to say, "What's all this mess on my broad-cloth?" sweeps all the flowers and stuff on to the floor, calls in Flute and Snout and proceeds to fold up the green tarpaulin. Oh, of course, it's a carpenter's bench: we are back in Quince's workshop again, and here he is himself in great dejection: "Haue you ſent to Bottoms houſe? is he come home yet?" The handicraftmen, jubilant by the end of the scene at Bottom's return, carry out the bench as they go—and with it all signs of the carpenter's shop.

SHAKESPEARE, with his crowded climaxes, must usually have written his last scenes for the full depth of the stage, with inset open. Certainly the fifth Act of *A Midsummer Night's Dream* is no exception. Two questions arise: when was the inset opened once more? and what was the furniture disclosed for the end of the play?

The answer to the first question must be "as late as possible." The stage-hands who have had an easy time for most of the evening, suddenly at the end of IV. i become feverishly busy. Dismantling bank and brake is no light task, and at the end of IV. ii they have also to dispose of the carpenter's bench carried through the curtain by the jubilant mechanicals. If the inset is to be opened at all in Act Five, it must be either at Quince's prologue or, if more time is needed, for the subsequent dumb-show.

As to the setting, it must be devised to give full point to the finale. Shakespeare's intention is vividly elucidated by the editors of the New Cambridge Edition of the play, both in Quiller-Couch's well-known ideal presentation, and in a note on the text. Both passages speak of a private perform-ance—in 'the great chamber' of an Elizabethan house—which the editors assign to 1598.

"For the last scene and the interlude of *Pyramus and Thisbe*," says Q,[1] "the hall should be filled with lights and company. That over, the bridal couples go up the great staircase. Last of all—and after a long pause, when the house is quiet, the lantern all but extinguished, the hall looking vast and eerie, lit only by a last flicker from the hearth—the fairies, announced by Puck, should come tripping back, swarming forth from cupboards and down curtains, somersaulting downstairs, sliding down the baluster rails; all hushed as they fall to work with their brooms . . ."

"It is to us manifest," reads the note,[2] ". . . that the exit of the fairies at Oberon's command was arranged in such a way that they seemed to be departing on their mission of consecration from chamber to chamber. . . . The performance was at night . . . and as Theseus and his court left the stage, the candles that illumined it were extinguished one by one until the only light that shone was the glow of the embers on the hearth. It was in this twilight, we believe, that the fairies made their entry, after Puck's prologue, streaming into the hall, and kindling their tapers at the hearth as they passed by it."

Now if these two passages give a plausible and satisfying impression of the private performance of 1598, it seems proper to ask how Shakespeare and his colleagues adapted the scene for the public theatre in the following year, for the Globe performance of 1599. The two essentials are the staircase and the fire: for the mortals must seem to go up to bed, and the fairies to follow them; and the fairies must kindle their tapers "by the dead and drowfie fier." The staircase is comparatively easy to rig in the inset: and no doubt the Chamberlain's Men made use of the upper stage on the second level—what Cranford Adams calls the "chamber"—for the final departure of the Court to bed, and the fairies' blessing of "each feuerall chamber" throughout the palace.

---

[1] M.N.D. (*New Cambridge Shakespeare*), Intro. xxi. (repeated from Quiller-Couch's *Shakespeare's Workmanship*).

[2] *Ibid.*, p. 151, note on V. i., 389-90. The note goes on to point out that the tapers were worn on the head, and draws an interesting comparison with *The Merry Wives of Windsor*, V. v. See also p. 98.

B

But what of the fire? Where, when and how was it kindled? And how was its presence made to seem appropriate? After our long sojourn in the wood, and a brief visit to Quince's house, there is good need to re-establish the atmosphere of the Duke's household. Shakespeare was adept at doing this kind of thing—whether elaborately, as in Capulet's busy preparations for a dance or a wedding and in the setting of Aufidius's house in Antium, or quite simply in Macbeth's feast to entertain Duncan.[1] So here the same kind of device can be applied: Act Five will begin with the henchmen under the tyrannical eye of Philostrate bustling in with fire-dogs and irons and logs, and building a fire in the very centre of the stage over the trap-door; the structure complete, all squat in a circle round it using their breath to kindle the flames: meanwhile in their midst the trap opens, and stage-hands below push up among the pile of logs a glowing flickering fire, and raise from "hell" a cloud of infernal smoke.[2] So as the music swells to a climax of triumphant welcome, Theseus is able to lead Hippolyta to his own fireside. If there are captious critics who take exception to a fire in June, Shakespeare is ready for them: for Titania earlier in the evening has informed us of the seasons being so much disturbed that

> hoary-headed froſts
> Fall in the freſh lappe of the Crymſon roſe—

and (if we accept an admirable emendation)[3]

> The humane mortals want their winter gere.

This midsummer fire proves in practice to be no irrelevant luxury. It gives the right setting for Theseus's famous reflection on the process of poetry: he stretches his hands to the warmth of the blaze and stares into the heart of the fire,

---

[1] *R. and J.*, I. v. and IV. iv., *Coriolanus* IV. v., and *Macbeth* I. vii.

[2] See Appendix, p. 130.

[3] Brae's emendation, *gere* (i.e., "gear") for *here*, discussed *ad loc.* in M.N.D. (*New Cambridge Shakespeare*), p. 114.

and the mounting smoke helps him give to "ayery nothing A locall habitation and a name." And when afterwards his guests spread themselves and sit round the front edge of the stage watching *Pyramus and Thisby* like the first row of the assembled company, the audience too warm themselves at the blaze and the whole theatre becomes a domestic circle looking across the embers, with a genial tolerance like the Duke's own, at the antics of simpleness and duty, and ready to amend with their imagination.

AFTER the mortals have gone up the great staircase to bed, the attendants snuffing the candles, Puck is the first to appear, jumping—through the trap—out of the fire itself. When the fairies have lit their tapers—with the help of the stage-hands—at the embers, they skip at Oberon's bidding up the great staircase to bless the best bride-bed. Puck returns into the fire as the inset curtain is pulled on a picture of Oberon and Titania mounting the upper stair. The illusion is over with the pulling of the curtain. The epilogue is polite convention.

3

THE MUSIC

*

THE problem of the settings being solved, the next question is the music. In no respect is the over-painting of Shakespeare's masterpiece thicker, and yet so skilfully has Mendelssohn used his brush and palette that many people take the picture as he left it for the original. His *Midsummer Night's Dream* is a work of genius, but it is not Shakespeare. The music, steeped in the colours of the Romantic age, makes use of the outline of Shakespeare's plot, but reinterprets the atmosphere, particularly of the fairy world, on which it lays special stress. Moreover, it is associated with a theatrical tradition quite foreign to the conditions of the Globe—the theatre of distant pictorial illusion, of footlights and spotlights, in which the audience sit detached and critical, gazing through the wrong end of a telescope at a remote tableau. You need only hear the opening chords of the familiar overture, and the memory conjures up a picture of gauze skirts, tinsel wings and the block-toed shoes of a ballet-dancer. As for the bridal march, it is—perhaps by the freak of fortune which has made it the best-known of all classical tunes—the most inappropriate prelude to Shakespeare's Act Five. No audience can recover from the shock of hearing music so familiar and so evocative of personal and often irrelevant associations, in time to listen to Theseus's pregnant sentences about the power of the imagination. It is an ironical paradox that nothing has done more than this artist's inspired music to obscure Shakespeare's artistry.

At the risk, therefore, of incurring a charge of perversity, the producer must set about exorcising Mendelssohn. It might indeed seem perverse, if there were nothing to put in his place. But when it is remembered that the supposed performance at the Globe was given in what has been called the golden age of English music, then the boot is surely on the other foot: to refuse to draw upon this great treasure of music, to prefer to first-rate music composed by Shakespeare's own contemporaries and fellow-countrymen the work of a composer from a different native climate and a different cultural age, seems an extreme form of cussedness which only unthinking habit can explain.

We must put once again the same question: what did they do in 1599? or rather—since no certainty can be reached on the point—what are they likely to have done? and how can we reconstruct a musical "score" for the play that would be both probable in the conditions of the Globe theatre and dramatically helpful in presenting the play?

Richmond Noble has thoroughly explored the special aspect of Shakespeare's use of song.[1] His method is to consider each play in turn, and his book is of great practical value to the producer. There is room for another such book dealing, on the same detailed plan, with the appropriate accompaniment for the plays of instrumental music and effects.[2] Noble draws his reader's attention to Shakespeare's increasing skill in making his songs serve a dramatic purpose, and cites *A Midsummer Night's Dream* as a turning-point in this respect. He is for confining the singing in this play—if we except Bottom's ditty—to Titania's lullaby in II. ii and the blessing-song of the finale. He rightly rejects a musical setting of Puck's opening interchange with the fairy in II. i and of Oberon's description of Titania's bank.

But the scope of his book does not include the rest of the music used in the plays: and it is a subject which needs

---

[1] Richmond Noble, *Shakespeare's Use of Song* (Oxford, 1923).
[2] Dr. E. W. Naylor in his *Shakespeare Music* (Curwen, 1912) shows the way by dealing with the detail of music cues in *Hamlet* and two other plays.

exploring.[1] It seems in keeping with all that we know of
Shakespeare's taste to suggest that he would have stood out
as far as possible for dramatic relevance. As a general
practice, a producer would do well to aim at using music
only where Shakespeare demands it: and usually, but not
always, we get an indication of what he wanted either in
the text itself or in the stage directions of Quarto and Folio.
Anything like the "background-music"—casually and sometimes, it would seem, almost accidentally employed—to
which we are nowadays subjected in the cinema, would
have been repugnant to Shakespeare. But incidental music
of a kind was familiar to the theatre both before and after
the date of the Globe production. The masque brought
music to the stage as early as the 1570's, and the oft-recurring
dumb-show was regularly accompanied by music. The
music that feeds Orsino's love or that which smooths the
pillow of the waking Lear, has each its dramatic purpose.
So in a different vein have the alarums and excursions of a
battle. But the flourish, the tucket and the sennet are often
evoked by the need to give dignity to an entry. Cranford
Adams tells us that the musicians were normally placed
behind a curtain of light texture in a gallery on the third
level of the Playhouse, close beneath the "heavens", and
quotes a pamphlet of 1631 which tells us that "the en-
curtain'd musique sounds, to give enter-breath to the
actors and more grace to their action." [2] To introduce upon
a stage without proscenium curtain a numerous procession
or a battle-array is a difficult task, and I have little doubt
that the Chamberlain's Men often felt the need for music to
give more grace to their action. Imagine in our play the

---

[1] Helpful suggestions will be found in Dr. E. W. Naylor's *Shakespeare
and Music* (1931), and in the articles on Music in *Shakespeare's England*
and the *Cambridge Companion to Shakespeare Studies*. But the producer who
seeks to recapture the methods of the Chamberlain's Men needs a
detailed examination of the crucial points in each play where Shakespeare
calls for music or other off-stage accompaniment.

[2] J. Cranford Adams, *The Globe Playhouse*, p. 322 f.

first entry of the Court amid embarrassed silence, or the stampede of a dozen choir-boys which represents the clash between the fairy King and Queen. These moments need music, if they are to avoid absurdity.

When we turn to consider what sort of music and what kind of musicians to employ, it soon becomes clear that *A Midsummer Night's Dream* presents a problem unusual among the plays of Shakespeare. The histories and most of the tragedies dictate the main quality of their orchestration, needing preponderantly the martial instruments, hautboys, fifes, trumpets, drums. The comedies are more likely to ask for chamber music: a chest of viols will feed Orsino's love and do for Portia's music of the house, while Feste will sing his airs to the lute; and *Tell me where is fancie bred* will be delivered with the strings by a solo voice supported by a "burden". In these two comedies at least, Shakespeare seems at pains to make his instrumentation plausible, to explain the presence of the musicians of his choice: and the task of the present-day producer is a simple one—of obeying the poet's instructions. But in the case of *A Midsummer Night's Dream* what *are* his instructions, what does he want us to do? Of whom does he think as making music in the wood? What is Titania's "music of the house"? The answer to this last question is there for the finding. When Titania wants a lullaby, she bids her fairies sing her asleep. When later in the play she calls for "muſick ſuch as charmeth ſleepe," why should she be thought to mean any other kind of music than before?

There are four good reasons for choosing to have the music in this play mainly sung; and not the prescribed songs only but the incidental music as well. Not one of these reasons amounts to a proof that this is what was done in 1599. All four together make it seem an inviting possibility. First, if the music is to sound "natural" and not man-made, by a strange paradox no instrument can be so telling as the human voice. Secondly, the finest music in that finest age of English music was mainly vocal: and Shakespeare writes of

music as a lover of his love, and speaks of "prick-song" as if
he knew it by experience. Thirdly, the madrigalist Thomas
Morley was known to Shakespeare and set at least one of the
songs in *As You Like It*—though not in madrigal form—to
music. *As You Like It* appears in Chambers's conjectured
chronology [1] as one of the plays for 1599-1600. And fourthly

—an accident of circumstance—there were for the Globe
performance choir-boys already in the playhouse. At least,
the fairies must have been borrowed for the occasion, just as
they were for *The Merry Wives of Windsor*, and presumably
they were Children of the Chapel Royal, or some such
accomplished and highly-trained singers. And if half the
choir-school were frolicking on the stage, why should not
the other half be carolling in the gallery aloft? Then indeed
for the court-scenes perhaps the whole choir would be available to make the music of the mortals louder in proportion
to their size.[2]

---

[1] Sir E. K. Chambers, *William Shakespeare*, Vol. I, pp. 270-1.
[2] It occurs to me that perhaps these choir-boys were another reason
why the play fell in 1600 out of the repertory. It would be difficult to
draw them from their regular occupation. And perhaps, too, their
presence was a nuisance in the tiring-house—the little eyases!

If then the choir-boys are to be made to sing for their supper, the same Morley will give the first hint of where to look for their music. It was Morley who assembled for publication—a year or two after the date of this Globe production—the celebrated collection of pieces by twenty-six master madrigalists known as *The Triumphs of Oriana*. These were settings of poems in praise of Elizabeth and have a common denominator in the refrain which, with a few variants in the detail of wording, ends them all:

> *Then sang the shepherds and nymphs of Diana*:
> *Long live fair Oriana.*

There is a musical similarity too, for the first of these two lines is usually delivered in solid harmony, and the *Vivat* is then treated in free almost fugal imitation.

Dover Wilson thinks it unlikely that *A Midsummer Night's Dream* would ever have been played before Queen Elizabeth,[1] and remarks upon the risk Shakespeare took in giving his fairy queen a title that was often by implication applied to his mortal sovereign.[2] It is perhaps questionable whether the Chamberlain's Men would have been so reckless as to make use of Oriana's madrigals in celebration of Hippolyta. Yet as an example of what is dramatically and atmospherically appropriate for the opening of the play, and well calculated to "awake the peart and nimble ſpirit of mirth", it is hard to resist the spirited outburst of John Bennet's

> *All creatures now are merry, merry minded.*

After the preliminary bustle of attendants strewing rushes and pages having their uniform inspected by the major-domo, the singers are heard in excited *staccato*—

> *See where she comes, see where she comes,*
> *Queen of all queens renowned—*

---

[1] M.N.D. (*New Cambridge Shakespeare*), p. 100.
[2] M.N.D. (*New Cambridge Shakespeare*), p. 103.

and so Theseus leads in his Amazon lady, the cynosure of every eye, to loyal cries of "*Long live fair Oriana.*" [1]

The same madrigal can be used later at the entry of Theseus and Hippolyta for the hunting-scene in IV. i. Here there is an even happier correspondence of dramatic fitness. For the words of the madrigal, in stirring our enthusiasm for Oriana's approach, ejaculate "*Yond bugle was well winded.*" The approach of the hunting-party is signalled by the winding of horns within, and it is tempting to repeat the horn-call as an interpolation between the phrases of the madrigal. [2] But more important even than this verbal correspondence between the dramatic situations of the madrigal and the play, and outweighing the inherent improbability of the use of Oriana's triumph to celebrate another queen, is the fact that the flavour of the music from its very opening phrase plants us at once in the Elizabethan age—not in a ballet of Mendelssohn, nor yet, another danger, in a pale semblance of ancient Athens.

The principle once established, the working out in detail becomes a search through an enchanting field of music; there can be no finality of choice, only different degrees of appropriateness. Another madrigal of the Oriana set can be used for variety to bring on the Court in Act Five. As for the fairies, the Elizabethan musicians seem to have been just as conscious of their nature as the poets. For wit and gaiety, one need go no further than Weelkes's five-part ballet *On the plains Fairy trains.* [3] It is no intrusion upon the atmosphere of Shakespeare's stage, if the singers tell us—

> *Nymphs begin*
> *To come in,*
> *Quickly, thick and threefold:*
> *Now they dance,*
> *Now they prance,*
> *Present there to behold—*

and we gladly yield them three hearty fa-la's of approbation.

---

[1] For the words of Bennet's madrigal, see Appendix, p. 114.
[2] See Appendix, p. 127.   [3] See Appendix, p. 117.

Titania's lullaby in II. ii asks for careful handling. The stage-directions of the Quarto make it appear that the song begins with the words "You ſpotted Snakes . . ." and continues over two long and elaborately shaped stanzas. There is of course no contemporary setting of the words in existence, and to find a ready-made melody which will correspond to this intricate pattern is virtually impossible. To set the whole song, it is necessary to compose a melody in imitation of the Elizabethan style. There is an alternative: by limiting the words to be set, it is possible to fit them to the cadence of a lullaby of Byrd. The original *Lullaby, thou little tiny baby* is a sacred song, but Byrd was as little inclined as J. S. Bach to keep sacred and secular music in separate compartments of his mind. The fairies, therefore, will sing to Byrd's music—

> Lulla, lulla, lullaby, lulla, lulla, lullaby,
> Neuer harme, nor ſpell, nor charme,
> Come our louely lady nigh.
> So good night, with lullaby.[1]

This departure from the instructions of the Quarto has dramatic justification. While Titania composes herself to rest, her court bestir themselves to protect her: each of her four gentlemen concerns himself (in a spoken couplet) with a particular danger, and a lady-in-waiting invites the nightingale to join in singing the Queen to sleep—

> Philomele, with melody,
> Sing in our ſweete Lullaby.

Then, and not till then—quite appropriately—the song begins.

To introduce the scene of Titania's dotage (IV. i), there are fit words and music in a beautiful slow-moving madrigal of Wilbye, *Draw on, sweet night.*[2] The night is indeed drawing on apace: within a hundred lines, Puck will be hearing the morning lark and bolting to ground at the sound of the Duke's hunting horn.

---

[1] See Appendix, p. 121. [2] See Appendix, p. 124.

Of the fairies' song in the finale, Richmond Noble treats at length in his book.[1] Oberon, he suggests, is to sing the first two lines—

> Now, vntill the breake of day,
> Through this houfe, each Fairy ftray.

Then the next twelve lines will be sung by the fairies on the stage: and the tune must be written for the occasion. Then Oberon resumes—

> With this field deaw confecrate . . .

NICK BOTTOM, among his other accomplishments, is also expected to sing, if only to wake Titania from her flowery bed. He has, as he says on another occasion, "a reafonable good eare in mufique," his preference being for the tongs and the bones. He must therefore be provided with a tune out of the many catches and whistles and popular airs of the day. This tune—let it be called for the occasion the "Tongs-and-Bones"—will be much hummed and whistled by the mechanicals at their rehearsals both in town and in the wood: Bottom will do his best to sing it through his Ass head in the presence of the sleeping Queen; and it will come to its fullest expression played on the flute by Peter Quince as accompaniment to the Bergamask at the end of the tragedy of *Pyramus and Thisby*.[2]

---

[1] *Shakespeare's Use of Song*, pp. 55 ff.
[2] Mention should perhaps be made at this point of the view expressed by Barclay Squire in *Shakespeare's England*, Vol. II, p. 24, who says that polyphony was unsuited to the stage. It is here argued not that the madrigal-accompaniment suggested in these pages for the play was the usual practice of the Chamberlain's Men, but that it was appropriate (and possible) in this particular case.

THERE is, of course, no finality about the details of this suggested score. The range of choice is so wide that there must be much other music as good or better for the purpose. But by giving specific examples, it is perhaps easier to prove the main contention that the Elizabethans themselves can best provide music for this play. A glance through the Oxford collection of madrigal verse [1] is enough to recall the everyday poetical background of the Elizabethan age. The musicians understood and felt with the poets, and a bar or two of almost any madrigal of the period evokes the same background, against which Shakespeare's play stands in relief. It is a dangerous folly to look elsewhere.[2]

---

[1] *English Madrigal Verse* (1588-1632), edited from the Original Song Books by E. H. Fellowes (Oxford, 1929).

[2] Granville-Barker in his preface to the play, published in the Players' Shakespeare, refers to Cecil Sharp's *Music for A Midsummer Night's Dream*, Simpkin, Marshall, 1914. This contains a preface in which "the whole problem, Mendelssohn dismissed, has been argued acutely and with authority." I have hitherto been unable to consult this work, in which Sharp argues for folk-music to supply the need.

4

THE COSTUMES

★

BUT what in the world did it look like, Shakespeare's crowded stage in 1599? What would we not give for a glimpse of the play in performance? To go straight to the crux of the problem—how are we to dress the fairies so as to fulfil Shakespeare's intention? There will be little point in banishing Mendelssohn, if the fairies are to look like the conventional pantomime figures of picture-stage and picture-book.

A good tonic and antidote for the traditional characterisation can be found in Q's stimulating introduction to the New Cambridge Edition, where he draws attention to the stanza of Spenser's *Epithalamiom* about "the Pouke" and "other evill sprights", and speaks of Shakespeare's "real Warwickshire fairies." [1] There is relevant matter, too, in Dover Wilson's anthology of *Life in Shakespeare's England*, under the heading of fairies. But in these revelations of fairy character there is no plain clue as to their appearance.

There are tantalizing hints, but no more, in the last act of *The Merry Wives of Windsor*, when Mrs. Page and her fellow-conspirators are busy with "properties and tricking for our Fayries". The prevailing colours are black, grey, green and white. They are all to be masked and vizarded—but this may be more to conceal their mortal identity from Falstaff than a necessary item of fairy attire. Alternative costumes are suggested for the fairy queen: Page will have her all in white silk; Mrs. Page means

> That quaint in greene, ſhe ſhall be looſe en-roab'd,
> With Ribonds-pendant, flaring 'bout her head.

---

[1] M.N.D. (*New Cambridge Shakespeare*), Intro., especially pp. viii-xviii.

Add to these the item in Henslowe's property-list for the Globe of "iij fares (fairies') gowne of buckrome"—the same material as worn by Falstaff's imaginary assailants on Gadshill (and therefore perhaps good for invisibility?). Yet all these hints get us almost nowhere, and a more fertile line of investigation is to be found in the text of *A Midsummer Night's Dream* itself, where Shakespeare, as so often, in an apparently incidental way, makes his intention clear.

Let us concentrate for a moment upon the scenes in which Titania is the principal figure. She is an imperious queen, surrounded by her court, whom she sends upon her errands and employs in offices. Four of her courtiers are endowed by Shakespeare with names and a hint of personality. They are all four males, Gentlemen of the Chamber—Monsieur Mustardseed, says Bottom, and Cavalery Cobweb—and their tasks, such as ladies would not be asked to tackle, include standing sentinel over her majesty's nap and killing a humble-bee on the top of a thistle. I doubt whether a dramatist of Shakespeare's time could have conceived a scene of a female monarch giving orders to a company of obedient male courtiers without the familiar image of Elizabeth arising in his mind: and it looks as if Shakespeare, cudgelling his brains for a lifelike picture of the Fairy Queen at home, chose the model nearest to his own experience: the model of course must be reduced to the fairy scale, and instead of Essex being packed off to deal with the Irish problem, Titania's retinue are charged to

> warre with Reremife, for their lethren wings,
> To make my fmall Elues coates.

Now if Shakespeare has thought of Titania's train in terms of the Elizabethan court, he has left a hint to make the imitation plausible. The fairies after all have their model in the play itself—the Athenian court. And not only have they plenty of opportunity of studying the fashion from glimpses of the four lovers in the wood by moonlight, but also it is plain from the last scene of the play that they are in

the habit of peeping through the windows of great palaces
to see when the coast is clear. One way then of introducing
some logic of style in the dressing of this play is to have the
fairy dresses a parody—deliberate on the part of the wearers
—of the dresses of the Court. The point can be discreetly
emphasized by making the first appearance of Oberon and
Titania in II. i a kind of echo of the preliminary ceremonial
of Theseus's first entry.

So after all we must begin by deciding upon the Court
fashion. In this play, is there any reason against an
unequivocally Elizabethan wardrobe? It is clear—from
a host of details, such as Capulet's doublet and Falstaff's
slops—that Shakespeare habitually worked out his themes
in terms of the life of his own day: nor in dress only, but in
every circumstance of daily life anachronism is his rule:
Capulet's household is a case in point, where an Italian
noble rules the domestic roost like any Stratford burgher: it
is part of the secret of his vitality. *Julius Caesar* should be
dressed as Granville-Barker in his Preface suggests, in a
compromise between classical and Elizabethan attire; but in
Julius Caesar Shakespeare is at pains to project the spirit of
Rome upon the stage. In *A Midsummer Night's Dream*, on the
other hand, Athens is nothing: the life of the city, its topo-
graphy, its atmosphere are nowhere indicated, and the
wood, as has often been said, is native Warwickshire: the
names of the characters are selected haphazard from
Plutarch; their behaviour remains pure English, and the
Quarto's speech-headings of *Duke* and *Dutcheſſe* seem to give
a truer flavour than *Theſeus* and *Hyppolita* for the revels of
Act Five. What need then to submerge the contemporary
and lifelike vivacity of the play in archæological bath-towels
and blankets? Because Oberon lays stress upon the Athenian
costume of Demetrius? "Thou ſhalt know the man," he says

to Puck, "By the Athenian garments he hath on," and Puck makes his mistake because Lysander too wears "weedes of Athens." Now what is the distinctive feature of Athenian garments that Oberon indicates to Puck? Does he mean, "You can't mistake him; he's not dressed like a Spartan or a Theban"? No: nor, of course, does he mean to distinguish him from an Elizabethan! Or does he suggest—does Shakespeare bother to work the point out at all?—that Demetrius is wearing city clothes, not country wear? For the purposes of the plot, all that is necessary, to make Oberon's meaning clear, is to dress both Demetrius and Lysander smartly, and both in the same style.

The positive advantage of Elizabethan attire is that it presents the three lovers and their ladies in the guise of the kind of young men and women whom Shakespeare was used to see at a respectful distance and to admire in the early stages of his writing career. Dover Wilson hits off the young men of the "sonneteering" period very well in a passage of his *The Essential Shakespeare*:

"Play after play at this period contains its party of dashing young bucks. They come abroad to see the great world in *The Two Gentlemen of Verona*, *The Comedy of Errors*, and *The Taming of the Shrew*. They seek to combine this with university studies in the last-named, or they found a little 'academie' of their own in *Love's Labour's Lost*. Or yet again, as in *The Merchant of Venice* and *Romeo and Juliet*, they are just men about the town or gentlemen about the court, revelling and roistering and chaffing each other. Almost always too, like young men of whatever rank or period, they hunt in threes. Mercutio, Romeo, and Benvolio; Berowne, Longaville, and Dumain; Antonio, Bassanio, and Gratiano; Petruchio, Lucentio, and Tranio—so persistent is the triangle that it is hard to resist a suspicion that the same triangle existed among the 'divers of worship' for whose eyes and ears they were primarily intended." [1]

Theseus, Lysander and Demetrius are another manifestation of the same trio. They speak with the same elegant

[1] *Op. cit.*, pp. 49 f.

extravagance of conceit and strained imagery, which is wholly characteristic of the period and has nothing to do with ancient Athens.[1] The Romans in *Julius Caesar* never use this language, because in that play Shakespeare is attempting something quite different: there he has steeped himself in the atmosphere of Plutarch's Rome, and it is astonishing how easily his style changes and how successfully he communicates the classical grandeur. *A Midsummer Night's Dream* never leaves England except for fairyland, and the courtiers are of a piece with all the gallants of his early period.

SHAKESPEARE's fairies then, peeping through the windows of the Duke's palace, saw some such shapes as these, and when they return to the wood, half curious half mocking, will try to imitate what they have seen. Their materials are inexhaustible; it only needs some skill and luck in choosing the right stuff for their pattern. Shakespeare himself drops some hints of their ingenuity in improvisation. The snake's enamelled skin is "weed wide enough to wrappe a Fairy in": the leathren wings of bats make coats for Titania's elves: the wings from painted butterflies serve as fans for Bottom's slumber. So the fairies begin to choose their own styles. Peaseblossom is attracted by a soldier's kit: the shape of his leaf gives the right military cut to sleeves and skirt; the helmet comes easily from the blossom itself; the greaves are an afterthought; and the flat leaf of an iris makes him a well-tempered sword-blade. It is he that is sent to war with the reremice, he that deals firmly with spotted snakes and thorny hedgehogs, he that stands aloof as sentinel for Titania and is overpowered by Oberon's braves. He too,

---

[1] So too the ladies can be recognized in Dover Wilson's next page when he speaks of Shakespeare's "mocking wenches"—a type which he invented, and reproduced with variations in one play after another.

by a simple transformation of speech-heading, receives Bottom's instruction: "Good Mounfieur, get you your weapons in your hand, and kill me a red hipt Humble Bee on the toppe of a thiftle: and good Mounfieur, bring mee the hony

bagge." He is for ever sharpening his blade on the sole of his foot. Cobweb has been fascinated by the spectacle of a bishop moving about the palace with downcast eyes and clasped hands. It is simple to rig up a clerical gown from his private store of dusty gossamer, and the petals of a white flower make good Geneva bands. He presides in an attitude of benediction over Titania's lullaby and keeps the beetles at bay; and is in his element scratching the head of the translated Bottom. Mustardseed is the most dandified of all,

having studied the style and antics of some Spaniardizing grandee like Raleigh. There is a touch of the Don in his yellow doublet and black slashed trunks, with a triangular leaf sprouting from his chin as a Castilian beard.   He and

Peaseblossom join Titania's maids of honour, whose grassy skirts have the square hips of the farthingale, to dance a roundel at the Queen's bidding. Alone of her four gentlemen, the enigmatical figure of Moth defies augury. To begin with, he is not a moth: otherwise, he would no doubt have little scruple in tearing the wings from painted butterflies to make his slops and sleeves of Elizabethan cut. But the editors assure us that he is a *mote*. "A moth it is," says Horatio of the appearance of the Ghost, "to trouble the mindes eye":[1]

---

[1] *Hamlet*, I. i. 112.

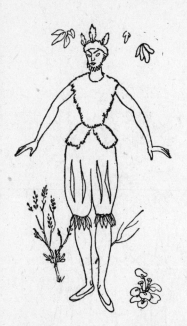

and Armado's little Moth is also just such a speck of dust.[1] And how the Chamberlain's Men would dress a Mote, is a trick imagination scarcely comprehends. Perhaps the best plan is to take a hint from *Love's Labour's Lost* and think of this Mote as a precocious and waggish page among the

Queen's attendants, bearing the same relation to Don Mustardseed as his namesake to Don Armado.[2]

For the rest, rushes make one suit, yew another, willow a third: there is one stout fairy in a cape of snakeskins, another decorates his cloak with bracken for lace, and one—most ingenious of all—has solved the problem of the ruff by wearing an inverted mushroom round his neck. The arms

---

[1] L.L.L. (*New Cambridge Shakespeare*), IV. iii. 158, note.

[2] There is a further puzzle about Shakespeare's conception of Moth: in the two scenes where the gentlemen are most prominent—III. i. 153 ff, and IV. i. 1-40—Bottom pointedly ignores him; so that Dover Wilson, in a note on the former passage, suggests that he had disappeared from the cast in 1598. The choice seems to lie between this arbitrary omission, which will lead to textual difficulties in III. i., or an attempt to tailor a suit for the character of Mote.

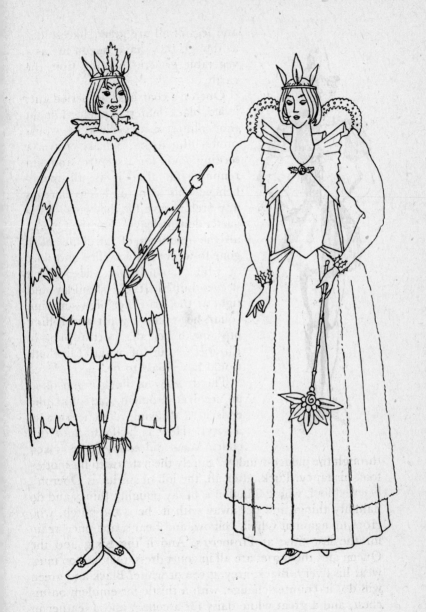

and legs of all are green like stalks, as though they have begun life as a vegetable growth shooting from the earth.

Oberon's coat has the period cut: faded black material makes him at times almost as invisible as his words profess him to be: a leafy crown, a seeding onion for a sceptre, and—to remind you that it is all make-believe—his arms and legs bare as any urchin, save for the order of the garter done in leaves. For the Queen, all the resources of fairyland have gone to weave her a bodice and skirt of white moon-beams. Her green sleeves puffed at the shoulder and tight at the wrist, her high-standing collar, her pointed waist and rolling hips make her the portrait not of Elizabeth, but of what Elizabeth would have liked to be.

The dressing of Puck is too often an unsolved problem, and sometimes ends in a drawing-room version of a satyr. How is he to fit into this court? What did *he* spy as he looked through the palace-window? Surely the jester with his motley took his fancy. Puck, after all, the lob of spirits, is Oberon's licensed fool, whose function is to say naughty things and do naughty things and get away with it: he is the patch, who crops up again at Olivia's elbow, and Lear's, and once again for the last time at Prospero's. And if the King and the Queen and the fairies are all in court dress, then he too must wear his livery. Black, grey, green or white? Black and green will do, in counter-change, with a thistle for emblem on his chest, and a great white daisy for a collar: and a feather in his hat; those bells might make him look altogether too much like a fool. Lord, what fools these mortals be!

For the mechanicals, there is no problem. They must be like the craftsmen of *The Shoemaker's Holiday*—with good leather jerkins and aprons and breeches. The tools and emblems of their trade, the sign of their profession, will help to make their identity plain and bring home their individual qualities to the audience—a rule for Quince, for instance, a bellows for Flute, and scissors and thread for Starveling. And for their play, the costumes and properties will be home-made fustian.

5

THE PLAY

★

HAVING removed, we hope, most of the over-painting, we may now stand back and contemplate Shakespeare's own picture. It is one of the most perfect examples of his poetic drama. The economy and insistent relevance of the writing is astonishing, in one who is often supposed to be extravagant and discursive in the exuberance of his genius. There is hardly a speech in this play that is off the point, if we hear it as it was meant to be heard, in Shakespeare's theatre.

Sit for a moment on the verge of this rush-strewn arena, and you will quickly find yourself subject to the poet's spell. The madrigal for "enter-breath" but reinforces Shakespeare's own first emphasis: *"see where she comes, see where she comes, queen of all queens renowned."* Every eye, including the Duke's, is turned upon the splendid figure of Hippolyta the Amazon; the boy, dressed in her somewhat exotic robes, has perhaps been instructed to use the hard-lipped speech and arrogant mien of the lady who rides to hounds. In a score of lines we hear of the approaching nuptials, have already a hint of night and the moon, and are stirred up with the Athenian youth to merriments. Then with no further ado, the play begins to move.

Deftly we are introduced to the lovers and their problem together. They stand in a triangle, Hermia up-stage at the apex, while Egeus—another Capulet or Brabantio—barks his complaints from one side of her and Theseus from the other is the gentle but firm arbiter of life and death. Burbage has an easy afternoon with this play,[1] but would make the most no doubt of the poetry to freeze poor Hermia's young blood—and that of any coy mistress who sat by her lover in the two-penny gallery. Hermia speaks up, with a prophetic touch of Cordelia. Lysander is swiftly sketched as the more dashing of the two suitors, with a mordant wit and the assurance of the lover who is loved in return: Demetrius incurs the odium of unscrupulous fickleness. Helena, the fourth of the quartet, is cunningly held in reserve, though Lysander's mention of her kindles interest before her entry.

Left alone, Lysander and Hermia have a brief lyrical duet comparable to the familiar set-piece of Lorenzo and Jessica, or the graceful quartet in *As You Like It*.[2] Then swiftly the plot is furthered with plans for elopement. When Helena is introduced, she strikes at once the note of eloquent and witty self-depreciation which makes her gawky plainness charming and prepares us to accept her unmaidenly pursuit of her faithless lover, which would otherwise be embarrassing, as graceful comedy. The part is beautifully devised for a boy to play: for a woman it proves in practice harder. By way of exposition, when the scene ends, we are left in no doubt that we shall meet this engaging foursome in the wood to-morrow night—and we look forward to the meeting.

WHEN Bottom appeared at the first private perform-ance of the play, Shakespeare must have suffered under Will Kempe's gags and gambits, setting on "fome quantitie of barraine fpectators to laugh." But now perhaps in 1599 in the public theatre, Robert Armin has taken over the part and shown proper appreciation of the

---

[1] If Theseus is his part. T. W. Baldwin (*The Organization and Personnel of the Shakespearean Company*, p. 271) assigns the part to Augustine Phillips, and gives Burbage Demetrius: he is thinking of an early performance, in summer, 1594, when Burbage was just being taken into the company as a permanent member.

[2] *M. of V.*, V. i. 1-22; *A.Y.L.I.*, V. ii. 89-117.

skill with which the comic scenes are written. How often since that day has traditional "business" obscured the simple outlines of Shakespeare's invention! How often has Bottom forgotten that he is a weaver in his pitiful ambition to prove himself a comedian! How seldom do we see a performance that is built steadfastly on the scaffolding of Shakespeare's words!

On to the empty stage, humming and whistling the "Tongs-and-Bones", come half a dozen hard-handed craftsmen, struggling under the burden of a carpenter's bench. The people and the furniture are enough to change the scene from high life to low. The business in hand is made clear at once—an "Enterlude, before the Duke, & the Dutches; on his wedding day at night". Two of the six are prominent at first: Peter Quince, the host and chairman, busy and confused with the laborious business of reading and writing; and Nick Bottom, the weaver, whose irrepressible enthusiasm keeps interrupting the chairman with advice and instructions. The clash of personalities between the two is good enough comic material to give dramatic unity to the whole scene. When he has heard his part described, "To the reft", says Bottom, and immediately returns to a contemplation of his own histrionic powers. "Now, name the reft of the Players," and still he has not finished dwelling on himself. Flute is the youngster of the party, with "a beard coming". He is romantically inclined and fancies himself as "a wandring knight", and is pathetically disappointed when he hears he is to play a woman. Yet when the time comes, he puts his soul into his playing. Starveling may reasonably be old and deaf—as befits the man in the moon—and threadbare and lean, as his name implies and as other Shakespearian tailors are. Snout can be tall to make a good partition between the neighbours, and to contrast with Snug, a very mouse of a lion. Little Snug is the butt of the party; for so he appears for a moment at rehearsal in the wood: certainly he is slow of speech and slow-witted, and there is a pretty irony in his request to have the Lion's part written because he is "flowe of ftudie", Quince, the manager and the brains of the company, is quick of tongue with a home-spun wit that can quiz Snug and humour Bottom. They are all good friends and all one in their admiration of Bottom, who must be a charming good-natured fellow for all his bounce, or they would not like him as they do. When Quince says crossly "You can play no part but Piramus", and Bottom goes off into childish sulks, there is general despondency until Bottom consents to undertake it. Thereafter all is excitement over the plans for rehearsal. We shall enjoy meeting this company too in the palace wood by moon-light.

It is a recurrent feature of Shakespeare's technique to sustain the interest of the audience by dropping hints in anticipation of good things to come. Already in this play we not only expect to meet the lovers and the mechanicals in the wood, but we look forward to the Interlude before the Duke and Duchess on his wedding-day at night. And with these delights in store, he opens yet another casket, all unseen and unexpected, and draws out treasure richer than any hitherto.

FOR it is now that the moonlit wood is created in the twinkling of an eye, and now we are led to the brink of expectation for the entry of the fairy courts. This opening dialogue fulfils other functions too: it makes a plain statement of the cause of dispute between Oberon and Titania, the mainspring of the fairy plot; and it gives us a pungent foretaste of "that ſhrewde and knauiſh ſprite, Call'd Robin goodfellow". The boy who played Puck would, I think, like Oberon and Titania, be one of the regular boy-actors of the company—it seems from the cast-lists of many plays that they could run to six—and not an imported choir-boy. He would be highly trained to play so exacting a part, and must be prepared to dance and mime his way through it with an appearance of spontaneity that could only come with gruelling practice. Here already he must neigh like a foal, and ape the spluttering gossip, and become a three-foot stool, a toppling aunt, and a laughing quire in rapid succession—a *tour de force* which will not succeed till it comes natural.

"*Enter the King of Fairies, at one doore, with his traine; and the*

Queene, at another, with hers." This simple statement in the Quarto brings the whole recklessness of Shakespeare's make-believe to life. Yet the King's opening words seem almost insolently contemptuous of the imagination that cannot "peece out our imperfections with your thoughts".

C

> Ill met by moonlight, proud Tytania—

he cries, serenely assured of his audience, and a clearing in
the wood is thronged with the rival courts ready to square.
It is, in miniature, like many another cross-stage wrangle in
the historical plays.

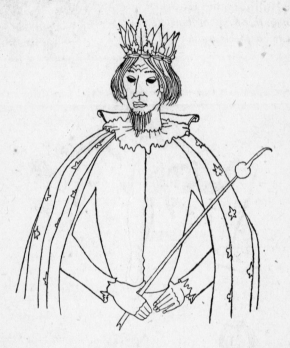

In considering Shakespeare's fairies, it is well not to forget
the material with which he was working—the boys of a
neighbouring choir-school. They were the same probably
who served for the last act of *The Merry Wives of Windsor*,
when they were required to be bogus—obviously bogus—
fairies, Falstaff the only victim of their illusion, the audience
in the joke. Catching such a fairy for his bride in the blind
man's buff, the foolish Master Slender complains that he has
been fobbed off with a postmaster's boy, "a great lubberly

boy". Falstaff himself perhaps in very early youth, before he
was page to the Duke of Mowbray, was such a choir-boy—
the time when he learnt his pastime of "hallowing and finging
of Anthemes". Can you not see him bland and cherubic,
looking to right and left as the Precentor rates the boys for
their naughtiness, and then under the fixed stare of accusa-
tion: "I would your Grace would take me with you: whom
meanes your Grace?" The species is after all not extinct: if
instead of following the sermon, you keep your eye on the
front row of the choir-stalls, you will see how eagerly
Shakespeare would fasten upon this stuff for the raw material
of his picture of fairy-life. That "who, I, sir? not I, sir! must
have been him, sir" look would be so easily convertible into
the other-world oddity that pops out from behind a bush,
starting and stopping like a lizard so suddenly that you do
not see him move but only know it by the change of position,
always apt to disappear and with a dose of fern-seed become
invisible.

The raw material then is a mob of boys, some cherubic,
some lubberly in appearance, all apt for mischief. What does
Shakespeare make of them? In the first place, he does *not*
represent them as children. Their small stature is not a sign
of tender years. They are "the little people", and therefore
the whole Court is smaller than mortal size: but everyone is
to scale and, as far as age means anything in fairyland, they
are all grown-ups. To them as to us the little Indian boy, the
cause of all the bother, is but a child. Any suggestion of the
pretty simplicity of childhood so often associated with fairies
is rudely dispelled by the first interchange of Oberon and
Titania with its sharp-tongued recriminations of adult
jealousy. Even Puck, with all his gratuitous mischief, never
speaks like a child, and—more significant—Oberon never
speaks to him as such. The courtiers too are grown-up [1] and
do their offices with the same solemnity as their mortal
counterparts. Everything of course is reduced to scale; but

---

[1] Possibly Moth is the exception; see above, p. 54.

it is man's work rather than child's play to hunt bats for their wings, to ward off owls and snakes, and to steal the honey-bags of humble-bees; there is an unromantic realism of practical resourcefulness about the added instruction:

> And for night tapers, croppe their waxen thighes,
> And light them at the fiery Glowe-wormes eyes;

and no nonsense of pretty tenderness in Titania's command to "pluck the wings, from painted Butterflies" (a touch of Queen Elizabeth about this order?): moreover a fairy would indeed need to be venturous, to seek the squirrel's hoard and fetch Bottom some new nuts. Fairy politics likewise are reduced to simple issues—a downright squabble for possession. There is a piquancy in seeing the King and Queen and their courtiers engaged in these trivial occupations with all the seriousness of their mortal models; but this kind of mock-heroic reduction in scale has been a never-wearisome commonplace of pastoral ever since Theocritus. There is in this case an added delight in seeing boys pretending to be grown-ups behaving unconsciously like boys—an effect which Shakespeare often achieved in another way, with his boy-actors playing Portia and Rosalind and Viola in boy's attire.

So if at this first appearance of theirs the fairies grow a little restless during Titania's long speech, standing on one leg, yawning and stretching, slyly winking at one another—with that discretion of inattentiveness bred of much suffering under sermons—then not much of Shakespeare's intention, I believe, is lost.[1] And it will be all to the good if, when at long last they are allowed to go, they break away in disorder with cart-wheels and tripping and tumbles, as if dismissed from a tedious parade: for a second we are allowed to see what these courtiers—and these actors—are like off duty.

---

[1] Puck's plain hint, however, must not be forgotten, that when the King and Queen square, "all their Elues, for feare, Creepe into acorne cups, and hide them there."

But Titania meanwhile has her work cut out. She and
Oberon and Helena and Theseus—and all those who are
entrusted with the long static speeches of Shakespeare—
must not faint by the way nor ever allow themselves to think

that he did not know his job, but must tackle them with the
assurance of a virtuoso who has both done his scales and
studied his score. Titania must understand every phrase of
this speech, must visualize each image, must not miss the
unexpected humour of the word "proude" as applied to the
flooding rivers, nor the half-comic pathos of the green corn
rotting "ere his youth attainde a bearde", nor the fun in the

phrase "the humane mortals", nor the swift change of mood in

> hoary headed froſts
> Fall in the freſh lappe of the Crymſon roſe,
> And on old Hyems chinne and Icy crowne,
> An odorous Chaplet of ſweete Sommer buddes
> Is, as in mockery, ſet.

She must study the music, too, so as not to misplace by unconscious and habitual stress of the metre the emphasis of the poet's deliberate counterpoint. And having done all this, she must then seem to forget it and give the illusion of each phrase coming "fire-new from the mint". This can be done if she sees every image afresh as it comes, with the poet's eye in a fine frenzy rolling, and uses here and there an eloquent gesture to turn his images to shape. The Elizabethan boy-actors were highly accomplished and highly trained, and the brilliance of the writing of his feminine rôles testifies to Shakespeare's confidence in their powers.

Titania's virtuosity is not merely an end in itself: it serves a dramatic purpose. If we listen to her, if she makes us listen to her, we have an urgent sense of the importance of the fairy quarrel. She moves us with a feeling of pity and concern for the distraught world, the victim of the immortal disharmony. The pity is kept beautifully within the framework of comedy, just as is the notion of Hermia's liability to the death-penalty, forgotten as soon as heard: here the description of nature's disorder is tempered by such lines as "the nine mens Morris is fild vp with mudde" and "the humane mortals want their winter gere",[1] but the general disturbance of the seasons and the little calamities that follow are cause enough for us all to wish for a quick and happy solution to the dispute.

Oberon too needs virtuosity, as he gives Puck his instructions to fetch the flower. His eye and his gesture must support the words to make all clear to the audience—the

---

[1] See above, p. 34, and note 3.

picture of himself sitting on the promontory, the mermaid
out to sea in front of him, the descent of the stars; then
suddenly Cupid flying between moon and earth, then
aiming at the Vestal, then the shaft "quencht" (the very
sound of the word does it) in the moon-beams; then the
whole vast scene shrinking to a microscopic focus upon the
"little weſterne flower." Now if Oberon sees this picture as
he describes it phrase by phrase, then the audience will
inevitably see it too. And this is what can be done on
Shakespeare's unlocalized stage. But with painted scenery
fixing us in the wood, it is hard, almost impossible, to make
this voyage of the imagination.¹

HAVING introduced the three strands of his pattern,
Shakespeare weaves them together with marvellous
ingenuity. It is a complicated plot, yet the mechanism
always runs smoothly, never for a moment creaks; with
Oberon's lighting upon the distraught Helena just when he
becomes possessed of the charm that can cure her trouble;
the subsequent tangle among the quartet, the ringing of the
changes between the four, the delightful comedy of Helena's
supposition that all three are conspiring against her; the
master-stroke of Titania's introduction to Bottom.

Always the illusion of the wood is kept before us. The
lovers help in this: Demetrius tries to scare Helena with
telling her she should not

> truſt the opportunitie of night,
> And the ill counſell of a deſert place.

Lysander confesses to Hermia, faint with wandering in the
woods, that he has lost his way. Both ladies have their

---

¹ So likewise, for instance, Tarquin's ravishing strides have much less
impact on our consciousness if the eye is preoccupied with a picture of
Macbeth's courtyard. (*Macbeth*, II. i. 55.)

moment of being all alone and can add much to the illusion by their expression and gesture of alarm. The stage, grown vast when open to its full depth, gives the sense of distance between different groups of characters, and of remote loneliness when one of them is alone. The queen sleeps on under her canopy, the lovers take their interrupted naps in front of the fore-stage bank. The hawthorn-brake, the clowns' tiring-house, serves also as cover for the invisible King and his jester-servant. What a playground for Puck! An imaginative actor will make it his own in no time; finding a snake—a dummy snake—hidden in the rushes, animating it with a startled jump, then knocking it on the head and tying it round his waist for a belt, or hanging it behind to feign a tail; or, when he is bored with Oberon's behests, balancing a bulrush on his chin; these are gratuitous but not irrelevant touches, for they illuminate the merry wanderer of the night, and the wood, the scene of his mischievous activities. And he will mimic the lovers or the clowns; there are plenty of hints in Shakespeare's text for his developing.

I do not understand why the four lovers are spoken of as a weakness in the play. They lack character, people say, and so are tedious. It is true or almost true that they lack character: but tedious they are not. Every time I have seen the play, I have looked forward to their long squabble, and seldom been disappointed; and there is much else to delight in too. Shakespeare has handled them with his unerring tact; and those who clamour for more character should be asked to specify what kind of people they would like in their place. It is not as if, even at the early stage when this play was first written, Shakespeare could not create character of a kind; Julia in *Two Gentlemen of Verona* is by no means lifeless. Nor by the same token—and the same example—was he embarrassed at the idea of giving a serious twist to "the Doue" pursuing "the Griffon". But surely there is a good reason for his deliberately avoiding the pit-fall of taking his young lovers too seriously—which some might say was the trouble

in *Two Gentlemen of Verona*. The fact is that what Shakespeare
wanted them for in this play was to make us laugh through
their experiences as victims of Oberon's magic and the
pranks of Puck. The preposterous switching of the men's
affections would be intolerable if the ladies made us feel too
deeply for them. So for his purpose Shakespeare did not
create a Viola whose tender feelings would wring our hearts
with her sufferings: rather he made his lovers more of the
emotional weight of Orsino and Olivia, who are superficially
treated perhaps for the like reason that they are the victims
of an equally preposterous situation arising from Viola's
disguise and her resemblance to her twin brother: we laugh
gently at the lovesick Duke and the bemused Countess in
Twelfth Night, and we follow the fortunes of this quartet with
the same kind of laughter—though more uproarious, since
they are persons of less dignity and social standing!

No doubt Shakespeare did not consciously ponder how
far he would use characterization. His treatment of the
lovers is an admirable example of the economy and insistent
relevance of his technique—an object-lesson in play-writing.
Every time they appear, it is the situation that he dramatises:
he is concerned with the progress of his story. From the start
he gives us the facts of the situation and wastes no time on
the underlying motives. Demetrius has thrown over Helena
in favour of Hermia: we are told the fact, we are not told
why. Egeus supports this "ſpotted and inconſtant man"
against Lysander as a suitor for his daughter's hand: we are
given no inkling of his reason. Theseus offers Hermia a
choice of three equally insupportable fates—death, the
cloister or Demetrius—and our reasonable protests are
ignored: it is "the Law of Athens". Once the complicated
dilemma is stated, the poet finds arising out of it a whole
series of situations which will project themselves into lively
dialogue. He learnt the art from Ovid, whose fertile invention
no prescribed circumstances could baffle: give him Theseus
and Ariadne, or Hero and Leander, or Pyramus and Thisbe;
he will describe the scene to you and put words into the

mouths of the actors, and the words will not go deep into motive and character, but they will be full of poetical vitality, and the reader's attention will never flag.

So when Demetrius and Helena first appear in the wood, we are reminded at once of their circumstances. No exposition could be more compact for this purpose than Demetrius's opening speech:

> I loue thee not: therefore purfue me not,
> Where is Lyfander, and faire Hermia?
> The one Ile flay: the other flayeth me.[1]
> Thou toldft me, they were ftolne vnto this wood:
> And here am I, and wodde, within this wood:
> Becaufe I cannot meete my Hermia.

The business of the scene is to excite the interest of Oberon, standing invisible behind, so that he will intervene on Helena's behalf. Her humiliating pursuit of her scorner is decorated with every artifice of conceit, allusion and hyperbole—so that what might be an intolerable situation proves delightfully amusing. There is plenty of room on this great stage for a good run: Demetrius would dodge her behind a pillar that is now a tree: and the groundlings in a close ring round the pair would doubtless cheer the boy-lady as she grew more and more out of breath in her fond chase.

Meanwhile all the gallantry in Oberon is stirred by the sight of this sweet Athenian lady who is in love with a disdainful youth. And pat at that moment Puck turns up with the little western flower. Oberon describes to us Titania's couch and declares his purpose:

> with the iuyce of this, Ile ftreake her eyes,
> And make her full of hatefull phantafies.

Then as natural sequel to the scene both he and we have just witnessed, he bids Puck take some of the juice and anoint Demetrius's eyes with it.

---

[1] Theobald's emendation of the Quarto "ftay . . . ftayeth."

It is at this point, I believe, that the inset-curtain at the Globe was drawn. It is the simplest way of indicating a change of locality, and the canopied bank, but just now described by Oberon, has its dramatic significance as being the objective of Oberon's malicious purpose: we know that if the Queen sleeps there, she will be in peril. The danger materializes at once: as "one aloofe"—Captain Pease-blossom—stands sentinel. Oberon appears behind and signals to his henchmen, who emerge from the hawthorn-brake with the stealthy tread of conspirators, overpower and gag the guard, and carry him kicking but not screaming from the scene. This is a moment which both choir-boys and audience will enjoy. The Queen is left at the mercy of her lord. As he streaks her eyes, his incantation is more mischievous than sinister: but the actor will do best to speak it in all solemnity; the humour is already in the words and needs no underlining.

No sooner has he gone than the other pair of lovers arrive. Shakespeare's business here is to get them to lie down to sleep at a sufficient distance so that Lysander on waking can see Helena rather than Hermia. Once again he makes a virtue of necessity: Lysander's pretty riddling and Hermia's no less pretty candour charm us round the awkward corner of an amorous good-night. Puck comes in bored and weary with foot-slogging through the forest; then at sight of the lovers recaptures all his animation, jumps to conclusions and squeezes the juice on Lysander's eyelids. Notice in passing the skill with which Shakespeare varies the music of the four-foot verse no less easily than he manages the pentameter: here in eighteen such lines we have boredom, surprised excitement, instant conviction, admiring compassion and ritual incantation. The poet in him never falters, and keeps the imagination of the audience in constant suspense of attentive delight.

Four lines of *presto* re-establish Helena's bootless chase of Demetrius: alone and out of breath, she descants in the

irony of ignorance upon Hermia's happiness, "wherefoere
fhe lies"; then catches sight of Lysander. There is a delicious
and calculated absurdity in his waking in time to echo her
cry with a rhyme. Again Shakespeare shows no concern for
character or motive: Lysander keeps up his reputation for
riddling, but his speech amounts to no more than an ornate
statement of the fact that he now hates Hermia and loves
Helena. That lady gives eloquent utterance to her indignation at what she takes for heartless mockery; but Lysander is
undaunted by her rebuke, aud so little troubled by his
conscience that his parting words to the sleeping Hermia are

> Of all bee hated; but the moft, of mee.

The vigour of this dialogue, all cast in the formal shape of
rhyming couplets, again reminds us of the stylized vitality of
Shakespeare's favourite Ovid. Hermia's nightmare, and her
terror and despair at finding herself alone, are no less
dramatic within their couplet frame.

WE are just beginning to relish the progress of this
entanglement in which the fairies with all good
intentions are making confusion among the mortal
visitors to their domain, when a distant hallooing and
whistling reminds us of the proposed meeting of our old
friends, Quince and company. Time for the clowns again,
is our first thought, and a little low comedy for light relief.
But Shakespeare, writing in the full flood of inspiration, is
content with no such humdrum motive. This visit of the
handicraftmen to the wood for their rehearsal is the preparation for his masterstroke.

There is the same economy and relevance in the writing
of this scene as of any other in the play: the business is to
rehearse the interlude which is intended for the Duke's
wedding-day; of this we are reminded in Quince's first

speech. The arrival of the mechanicals gives new life to the wood and indeed extends the expressiveness of the stage and its furniture. They carry lanterns and peer about them so that the darkness is more fully felt: one shudders with the chilly night air, another whistles (the Tongs-and-Bones) to keep up his spirits; Snug at least, who is to play the Lion, is much afeared of the dark and, supposing every bush to be a bear, clings on to the skirt of his big friend Snout's coat. But Quince decides it is a marvellous convenient place: there is a green plot for their stage, and a hawthorn-brake for a tiring-house, to cover their exits and their entrances.

The discussion of ways and means which precedes the rehearsal is in itself very funny—Bottom raising his knotty question just to show how cleverly he can answer it, the long jest about the Lion a slowly-gathering *crescendo* of laughter at the expense of little Snug, the allotment of the parts of Moonshine and Wall, both important to prepare us for the sequel in the last Act. But there is another reason why both rehearsal and performance are interesting, and when we come to the play itself we shall find cause to think that Shakespeare did not intend us to miss the point. Humble amateurs as they are, these six men are after all discussing the difficulty that confronted the Chamberlain's Men with every play they presented; how namely to create illusions with inadequate means. It is the old problem that Shakespeare almost defiantly tossed back to his audience in *Henry the Fifth*, how "with foure or fiue moſt vile and ragged foyles" to present Agincourt. "Peece out our imperfections with your thoughts", he cries; "for 'tis your thoughts that now muſt deck our Kings". And Theseus in this play, while *Pyramus and Thisby* is taking its absurd course, is at pains to lecture his bride on the need to amend with the imagination. Meanwhile even at the private performance of *A Midsummer Night's Dream* in the great hall of some nobleman, much more on the stage of the Globe in the afternoon, Shakespeare shows a delightful and characteristic recklessness in introducing Quince's poser of how "to bring the Moone-light into a chamber." Often enough he gets fun out of the situation of boy pretending to be girl pretending to be boy.[1] Here there is a like effect, with an actor in broad daylight pretending to be in a moonlit wood, and discussing how to get the illusion of moonlight indoors! There is satire here directed against the practice of prologues, and critics are quick to decide that Shakespeare is mocking the absurdities of stage convention, especially as the rival companies use it; but it is well to defer decision till the end of the play, before we judge which side Shakespeare is on, that of the actors or that of the audience. It may even be that with his habitual objective and unbiassed sympathy he will remain neutral, with a friendly eye to both.

Meanwhile they are ready to proceed with the rehearsal and—oh rich!—at that moment Puck pops up out of the ground right in the midst of them, alert for any kind of mischief. He reminds us that we are "So neere the Cradle of the Fairy Queene". She has been lying in full view all the time, but on this vast stage—with the emphasis centred elsewhere—it has been possible to forget her. Perhaps even now we do not realize the significance of her presence, and I think that Shakespeare does not mean Puck to realize either. His translation of Bottom is a mere spontaneous prank; he has no commission from his master to engineer the accident of Titania's waking. Oberon later confesses that it turns out better than he could devise; Shakespeare, in fact, is a more cunning deviser even than Oberon.

In Bottom's brief absence Flute keeps the ball rolling: throwing everything into his part, in his youthful enthusiasm he would speak the whole of it at once if Quince did not pull him up. He gives Pyramus his cue again, and Bottom reappears with the Ass head. Puck's six hectic lines, in pursuit of the dismayed craftsmen, are another virtuoso

---

[1] Most piquant of all is Cleopatra's indignation at the thought that if she were taken captive to Rome, she would see "Some ſqueaking Cleopatra Boy my greatneſſe." (*A. and C.*, V. ii. 219.) Oh for an afternoon at the Globe to hear a boy give its full flavour to this line!

piece—the problem being to imitate with movement first,
and then with intonation, a horse, a hound, a hog, a headless
bear and a fire; and then to recapitulate with both together;
and end up out of sight. Bottom (*solus*) is in spite of the
Ass head gloriously in character: "This is to make an aſſe of
mee, to fright me, if they could . . . I will walke vp and
downe heere, and will ſing that they ſhall heare I am not
afraide." And sing he does, with a reasonable good ear in
music, to his favourite tune of the Tongs-and-Bones.

"What Angell wakes me from my flowry bed?" It is the
masterstroke—all the better that we have seen the process
before with Lysander's waking—and it will never fail to
bring the house down. More than that, it is the perfect
blending of comedy and romance—as Dowden observes in a
fine passage on the play[1]—giving new life to both elements.
Even Bottom's commonplace ribaldries are dramatically
justifiable, for there is a purpose in emphasizing his coarse
fibre at this moment as the extreme contrast to Titania's
airy quality: it is the mortal grossness which it is her pleasure
to purge.

---

[1] Dowden, *Shakespeare's Mind and Art*, p. 361.

The Gentlemen of the Chamber—being also children of the Chapel Royal—will not take the passion of their Lady too seriously. True, they are startled at their first sight of her paramour, and their salutations are timorous and tentative, but as they gain confidence their approach to Bottom, blindfolded with the Ass head, is for all the world like a game of hoodman blind, his flailing arms falling heavy on each elf in turn. Titania, with her return to stately verse, intervenes before the fun becomes too riotous; and though Bottom so far forgets himself as to bray in the Queen's presence, the cadence as she leads him off, his tongue tied with a truss of hay, is in a vein of lyrical romance.

The episode of Titania's meeting with Bottom is rounded off by Puck's lively narrative: here is his chance to "ieaſt to Oberon, and make him ſmile". It is a great opportunity, if Puck is up to his job; woe betide him if he funks it. Often one hears the speech thrown away in an unintelligible gabble, accompanied by the moppings and mowings and physical jerks traditionally associated with Shakespeare's clowning. Yet the appropriate movement and gesture is almost dictated by the text. He begins to recount the scene which he and we have just witnessed, and he has the same stage-furniture for his version. So first he indicates the bower, with what suggestion of the royal forty-winks he thinks fit; then he marks out the stage, "this greene plot"; then he takes off Bottom with mischievous mimicry of his Pyramus; then points to the brake, and shows us how he fixed the Ass's nole on his head; next he skips across the stage to give us the simpering of Flute's Thisby; then, with all the pride of the impresario, "and forth my Mimick comes." It is Puck-Flute-Thisby who registers appalled dismay at the spectacle of the translated Bottom. So far all is easy—if the actor has practised long enough to make his timing seem spontaneous. What follows is harder—a full-blown simile to represent the terrified stampede of the crew of patches. Puck must not shirk this, nor hope to get away with a shapeless gabble. The unlocalized stage helps him; for he must now break

away from the scene in the wood, and confront us with a wholly different picture: he has failed if we do not see it— first the furtive creeping of the fowler, and the unsuspecting game, then the gun's report (a clap of the hands immediately after the word), then (with broad gestures of both arms—a

right and left—taking in the whole canopy of the Heavens, and the voice rising to a climax on the word "ſweepe") the scattered flight of the frightened birds. No sooner is this picture revealed to us than he must pick up his story, return to the green plot, and mimic the helter-skelter of the mechanicals; and so back to Bottom left alone, and the delicious absurdity of Titania's waking.

It is a great opportunity, but it needs the adaptability of the unlocalized stage to bring it off; and an audience ready to see pictures through their ears.

OBERON and Shakespeare do not pause long to gloat over the success of their scheme. They return at once to the lovers, and for the next half hour the play is concerned wholly with their entanglement. Whether or not the length of this development is beyond Shakespeare's original intention, whether Chambers is right in his suspicion that the whole passage from Hermia's re-entry to her indignant chase of Helena off stage is "later work", certainly there is no danger of tedium in this final version—with such skill and versatility does he "holde the fweete ieaft vp." It is like an exciting mixed-doubles match at tennis, with the

ball sometimes passing diagonally, sometimes down the side-lines, now lobbed to the back of the court and now smashed at the net: only there the comparison breaks down, for none of the four can be certain who is his partner, and Helena at least has the feeling that she is countering all three at once.

As a preliminary Demetrius must be made to fall asleep: he is shown pursuing Hermia and being soundly rated by her, for she supposes that he has murdered Lysander. At sight of them, Puck realizes his mistake. "This is the woman", he says, holding the seat of his trousers as he follows Oberon under cover of the brake, "but not this the man." (Take

heed, sirrah; the whip!) When Hermia leaves him, Demetrius, tired of his thankless suit, resigns himself to sleep.
Oberon sends Puck to remedy his mistake by fetching
Helena, and meanwhile proceeds to charm the sleeper's
eyes "againſt ſhe doe appeare". Puck is swifter than the
wind upon his errand, and returning settles down with
relish to watch the outcome: "Lord, what fooles theſe
mortals bee!" he cries, a line well tuned to the chuckling
scorn of the boy-actor. Shakespeare means him to whet our
appetite too by telling us what to expect:

> Then will two, at once, wooe one:
> That muſt needes be ſport alone.
> And thoſe things do beſt pleaſe mee,
> That befall prepoſt'rouſly.

The scene opens with marked formality: Lysander and
Helena address each other in parallel stanzas of six lines.
The reason may be to make the task of the boy-actor easier:
when Romeo and Juliet love at first sight, the pattern of
their dialogue is as formal as the dance in which they are
engaged. Here there is another reason too: the preposterous
volte-face of Demetrius under the influence of the love-philtre
would make realism intolerable. The fact of his change of
mind is told, without explanation or comment, in couplets
of Ovidian grace.[1] Helena's reaction to the long-desired
protestations of her beloved comes as a delightful surprise—
the best kind of surprise which makes you say "Of course!
that is just what we ought to have expected." She does not
take him seriously, and thinks that he is conspiring with
Lysander to make a fool of her. The boy who plays her

---

[1] It is unlikely that in the midst of this meticulous formality, there
should be no rhyme to Lysander's

> Demetrius loues her: and he loues not you.

A line must surely have dropped out here, and I suspect that Shakespeare
repeated his effect of a previous scene, and that the missing line is the
first of the waking Demetrius's speech, an indignant protest of which
the sense—let me not be so impertinent as to emulate the *expression* of
the poet—would be something like "What nonsense do I hear, as I
come to!"

should not miss the effect of the triple rhyming—once to round off her own speech, a second time to snub with finality the glib couplets of Lysander:

> Neuer did mockers waſte more idle breath.

Hermia's entry is equally formal in expression, and Helena's misinterpretation

> Lo: ſhe is one of this confederacy—

gains much point from the rhyme. Thereafter, as she rounds on her schoolfellow, the long sequence of blank verse begins which Chambers ascribes to Shakespeare's later manner. Whatever the secret of its conception, the change of style has good dramatic point; for now we pass from the preposterous motiveless facts to the natural and spontaneous comments of the victims, and are asked to sympathize first with one, then with the other of the two poor females in their bewilderment.

At first Helena makes all the running. There is no physical action, but a marvellous energy and vivacity in the words: the actor need but follow the shifting moods, and pitch and tempo and emphasis will suggest themselves. She is really affecting and pathetic in her appeal to the memory of her school-days—pathetic within the framework of tragi-comedy, suggesting Ovid again:

> Wee, Hermia, like two artificiall gods,
> Haue with our needles, created both one flower,
> Both on one ſampler, ſitting on one cuſhion,
> Both warbling of one ſong, both in one key;
> As if our hands, our ſides, voyces, and mindes
> Had bin incorporate.

There is a pungent logic in her attack on Hermia in her next speech, and the vigour of her denunciation of all three becomes comic only because we know that she is the victim of delusion. Her threat of desperate flight brings physical movement to reinforce the mounting excitement of the scene. Lysander runs after her, she brushes him aside: Demetrius braves his rival, Hermia interposes, clinging to her love:

with sword drawn, Lysander recoils from the thought of doing her physical violence, contenting himself with declaring roundly that he hates her and loves Helena.

"O mee, you iuggler!" As Hermia advances upon her school-days' friend, the turn of the tide is irresistible comedy. For the jealous recriminations of comparative stature, and the Billingsgate of puppet and maypole, together with Hermia's murderous assault—I believe boys can do this sort of thing as wholeheartedly as Shakespeare could wish. An admirable touch when Helena offers to bear her folly back to Athens, "ſo you will let me quiet goe", is Hermia's brutal calling of the bluff: "Why? get you gon. Who iſt that hinders you?" and there is shrewd satire in the confession "She was a vixen, when ſhe went to ſchoole", coming as it does so soon after Helena's romantic description of "All ſchooldaies friendſhippe, childhood innocence." The parting shot, "my legges are longer though, to runne away", gains greatly from a stage that has space for her to prove her boast.

But the scene cannot fail, on any stage: I have never seen it do so. It is a *tour de force* of sustained vitality, comparable in this respect with some of the greatest long scenes in the canon. It has of course the limitations of a lightweight theme, but the choice of theme is deliberate and Shakepeare's artistic tact makes him stay within the adopted framework. It gains something in the climax from the mobility of the Globe stage and the gusto of the boy-actors, and it demands from Helena a relish of her lines and the power to communicate that relish to the audience.

IT now begins to be time to think of the unravelling of the tangled skein. This is after all a comedy and at present we have two young men prepared to fight it out to the death in the wood, and two young ladies at large on a similar errand, and the Queen of the Fairies enamoured of an ass.

All which the unrepentant Puck esteems a sport. Oberon, however, in spite of his rather drastic method of educating Titania, has worked, as far as the mortals are concerned, with the best of intentions throughout. He now decides

quickly to take all possible steps to prevent calamity and restore peace and happiness ever after—"With league, whofe date till death fhall neuer end". Two things are needed—fog to keep the lovers apart, and an antidote for Lysander. Puck must deal with both, while he himself comes to terms with his Queen.

Shakespeare is in a hurry to wind up his plot, for his last Act is already booked for the Clowns' play at the Duke's nuptials. He therefore deftly communicates his urgency to Puck, who points to the approach of Aurora's harbinger. One interesting piece of spirit-lore is introduced at this point,

as if Shakespeare felt the need of exalting Oberon as he
moves towards the solemnity of the finale. Puck trots out
the familiar theme—so tragically presented in *Hamlet*—of
ghosts retiring at the first sign of day. Oberon counters with
the proud assertion that fairies are "ſpirits of another ſort",
and that he himself has often stayed up after his bedtime—

> And like a forreſter, the groues may tread
> Euen till the Eaſterne gate all fiery red,
> Opening on Neptune, with faire bleſſed beames,
> Turnes, into yellow golde, his ſalt greene ſtreames.

All the same, he adds, we had better hurry: and off he goes
to find Titania.

Puck is left to bring down the fog; and it is, I suppose, no
harder to create fog in daylight than it is to bring down the
night. Much will depend on how the lovers simulate their
blind stumbling. Meanwhile Puck gives a good start with
his sinister little incantation, whereby for a moment he is
positively alarming:

> I am feard in field & town.
> Goblin, lead them vp & downe.

The rest of the scene is a further test of the actor's virtuosity.
First he must imitate the accents of Lysander and Demetrius,
then give us the last ounce of humour in

> Yet but three? Come one more,
> Two of both kindes makes vp fower—

and

> Cupid is a knauiſh ladde,
> Thus to make poore females madde.

Then when he has composed them all to slumber in the
inset, he must catch the varied music of the incantation,
followed at once by a wild whirling dance-rhythm, as he
plunges below ground:

> Iacke ſhall haue Iill:
> Nought ſhall goe ill:
> The man ſhall haue his mare again, & all ſhall be well.

I F there is to be a break in the continuity of the play, the interval must presumably be at this point. It has already been suggested that there is no dramatic purpose to be served by the interruption. To make it possible, the lovers must sleep in the inset, two on the Queen's cradle, two

beneath the hawthorn-brake. Nothing is lost thereby; indeed, it is a positive gain to have Titania's dotage enacted in front of the fore-stage bank.

Some bars of Wilbye's madrigal to the words "*Draw on, sweet night*", reassert the mood at once, and remind us also of Aurora's harbinger and the regretful thought that this magical night must have an end. If the liberty is taken of writing Peaseblossom for Cobweb, the soldier rather than the cleric will be sent as highwayman after the humble-bee—

your honey or your life! There is anyway a muddle in the
text as we have it, and Cobweb is left on second thoughts—
appropriately—to scratch. The fairies greet the suggestion of
Tongs-and-Bones with shrill highbrow laughter—they are
after all trained musicians—and their mistress hurriedly
changes the subject. When they have vanished right and
left, and down into the trap, the focus is contracted to the
sculptured group of the Fairy Queen with the Ass head in her
lap—a timeless masterpiece, that dwells for ever in the
mind's eye.

Whether from his sense of urgency, or to spare Titania
humiliation in front of us mortals, Shakespeare skips over
the solution of the dispute in a brief narrative from the lips
of Oberon. It appears that everything was settled to the
King's satisfaction at a meeting "of late, behinde the wood",
and when the Queen wakes, no mention is made of the little
Indian boy, nor do we hear of him again in the sequel. His
function in the plot is purely mechanical, to set the quarrel
going; and nowhere is there any indication that Shakespeare
intended him to appear on the stage; if we judge by his per-
functory dismissal, it seems that the poet relies on our short
memories and the proverbial "out of sight, out of mind".
Oberon must not miss, nor the audience either, the beautiful
conceit of the humiliated flowers in Bottom's coronet:

> And that fame deawe which fometime on the buddes,
> Was wont to fwell, like round and orient pearles;
> Stood now within the pretty flouriets eyes,
> Like teares, that did their owne difgrace bewaile.

There is an atmosphere of solemn mystery as Diana's bud,
the fitting antidote to Cupid's flower, releases Titania from
the "hatefull imperfection of her eyes". Oberon calls for
silence, then, while Robin takes off the Ass head, music to
> ftrike more dead
> Then common fleepe of all thefe fiue the fenfe.[1]

No mortal eye must witness the ritual dancing of the royal

---

[1] Again it is Theobald who corrects the unintelligible misprint of the
Quarto.

reconciliation. We hear of Oberon's purpose to dance in the Duke's house to-morrow, and "bleſſe it to all faire proſperitie". Suddenly Robin cocks an ear: he has heard the morning lark. Oberon, forgetting his former boast, turns to Titania with words of haunting beauty:

> Then, my Queene, in ſilence ſad,
> Trippe we after nights ſhade.

We almost see the edge of darkness travel across the stage like the shadow of a cloud racing over the fields. Puck, watching them go, is startled out of his wits by the sound of a mortal horn: he plunges to ground by his familiar trap-door.

THE coming of the dawn has already been described. It is perhaps worth pointing out that the hunting-scene which brings it on the stage is the logical choice for Shakespeare's purpose—none the less a stroke of genius for being almost inevitable. His business is to wind up the story of the lovers with a happy solution of all their troubles in as short a time as possible, so as to have the stage clear for his last Act, already planned in full. The solution needs of course the presence of both Theseus and Egeus; and it is a singularly astute invention that brings them into the wood in time to see the lovers wake from their slumbers. There is only one circumstance of daily life that can lure a Duke into the woods at sunrise—a hunting-party. Shakespeare's lightning imagination sees at once how Hippolyta the Amazon can help here. "*See where she comes, see where she comes,*" chant the choir, "*queen of all queens renowned*"—with a new costume, a saucy riding-habit, that together with the men's hunting-boots, and some spears and bows, makes the occasion clear at once. A discreet hamper containing a stirrup-cup will give even the pages a relevant occupation.[1] It is to establish the effect of this early-morning hunting-party that Shake-

---

[1] See Appendix, p. 128.

speare has given to Theseus and Hippolyta those delightful
speeches about the music of the hounds. Once again the
words are no idle ornament but the poet's magical creation
of the atmosphere in which his scene is to be played. Gone
is the moonlit bower of Titania: instead we have "the
vaward of the day": we hear of "the weſterne vallie", where
the forester is to uncouple, and of the neighbouring moun-
tain-top: the drooping ears of the Duke's hounds "ſweepe
away the morning deawe". The impression of the freshness
of the morning is reinforced by Theseus when, on seeing the
lovers, he suggests

> No doubt, they roſe vp earely, to obſerue
> The right of May.[1]

The scene thus surely set, and the lovers wakened from
their dreaming by the matter-of-fact sound of the horns, the
business itself is quickly dispatched: Egeus renews his demand
for justice, Demetrius recants with as little explanation as
ever—"I wote not by what power (but by ſome power
it is)"—and the Duke decides without more ado to overbear
Egeus's will. All three couples are to be married in the
Temple, by and by. Meanwhile "our purpoſ'd hunting ſhall
be ſet aſide". It has indeed served its turn, scattering the
rear of darkness thin, the illusion of the fairy-haunted night.
An epilogue of pretty bewilderment, and the quartet of
lovers, in the may-morning of their youth, go skipping after
the Duke to the Temple:

> And by the way let us recount our dreames.

THE stage is empty. But no—there is Bottom stirring
from his more than common sleep. How easily Shakespeare has hidden him all this time right in front of
our noses, while the emphasis has centred round the lovers
in the inset. His speech has the cunning blend of realism

---

[2] I.e., "the rite of May."

and deliberate clowning that Shakespeare knew so well how to mix.[1] "Me thought I was, and me thought I had . . ." good miming, as he feels for his snout and his hairy ears, makes out of the transition from anxiety to relief a triumphantly comic realism: then the clown plays un-ashamedly to the groundlings with "But man is but a patcht foole, If hee will offer to fay, what mee thought I had." The Pauline travesty is likewise an appeal to the gallery: it is straining a point to suppose with the New Cambridge Editors that, as Bottom was a weaver, he may possibly be "of a Puritanical turn of mind".[2] I have looked in vain for other indications of this intention in Shakespeare's creation of the character. But when he is looking for superlatives to do justice to his dream, the familiar phrases of the Bible rise to his lips; only, being a clown, he gets them wrong. The resilient inventiveness of his conclusion is perfectly in character, and the Cambridge editors quite rightly point out that "at her death" means "at Thisby's death".[3] The Duke and Duchess are in fact to be treated to the Ballad of Bottom's Dream, at the end of the play—a hint which can be developed in rendering the Bergamask.[4]

As Bottom departs for Athens, the inset curtain is pulled, and the dismantling of the fore-stage bank to reveal the old carpenter's bench tells us at once that we are back at Quince's. All here is gloom—"the Play is mard. It goes not forward. Doth it?"—and the despair of poor Flute is most touching of all, with his naive admiration of Bottom's histrionic powers, and his assurance that the Duke would have given him a handsome pension of sixpence

---

[1] Macbeth's Porter uses it with no less successful effect in a tragic setting.

[2] M.N.D. (*New Cambridge Shakespeare*), p. 137.

[3] *Ibid.*, p. 137.

[4] See below, p. 102.

a day—"he would haue deferued it". I cannot believe that
the speech-headings are right which attribute to him the
correction of Quince's misuse of the word "Paramour".
The shocked pedantry of the correction is much more like
Quince himself, and I would give the malapropism to
Snout.

Bottom's return speaks for itself: "Mafters, I am to
difcourfe wonders—but aske me not what . . . I will tell you
euery thing right as it fell out—Not a word of mee. . . . All
that I will tell you is—that the Duke hath dined." The
bustle of preparation and the last-minute injunctions are the
best possible appetisers for the "fweete Comedy" to come.
The handicraftmen carry the bench with them as they go,
leaving the stage bare as a clean canvas for Shakespeare's
last picture. But the metaphor is the wrong one: for there is
nothing of the painter's distant tableau in Shakespeare's
method: and it is to partake in a social gathering that we
are now invited as the Duke's guests.

THE discussion of Act Five in the New Cambridge
Edition,[1] which suggests that the text was revised
wholesale by Shakespeare in 1598 and identifies
certain remarkable passages as belonging to this later
revision, is both ingenious and persuasive, but irrelevant to
the present purpose, which is to contemplate the finished
product: the text of the Fisher Quarto is that of the prompt-
book used for the 1599 public performances. We assume
that that text is—at the lowest estimate—not inferior in
artistry to its predecessors, and it seems likely that the
manuscript handed to the printer satisfied Shakespeare
himself and his colleagues as better than any other version
of his play then existing. This is not the same as saying that

---

[1] Pp. 80 ff. and 138 ff.

he went out of his way to prepare a text or to correct the proofs; but it is needless to suppose that the printer had anything else than the best rough copy available.

What then are we to make of the finished product? How is this last Act to be related to the rest of the play? Where is that economy and insistent relevance which has been so remarkable in the first four Acts? The plot is over and the tangled skein wound up. It is true that we have been led to expect the performance of the mechanicals' play; true also that the fairies have an appointment in the Duke's palace at midnight. These two issues must have been foreseen from the beginning: they are both the commonplace of wedding-plays—an Interlude, and the blessing of the married pair. And I suppose that the poet, faced with the problem of celebrating a wedding, set busily about his usual game of turning necessity into opportunity: the masque should provide his clowns with material—and not only in the finale, but all through the play—and the fairy-scene should round off the evening with enchantment. But what of the mortals? Are they to be merely passive spectators of the antics of the clowns? Well yes, almost. The lovers are neglected: those two eloquent ladies never speak at all, and their swains are but the mouthpiece of anonymous comment: no moral is drawn from the stealthy love of Pyramus and Thisby to bear on the similar predicament of Lysander and Hermia. Shakespeare turns away from the vista of possibilities opening in this direction: this would be irrelevant to his main-stream of thought, and he has, as we have seen all through the play, an admirable strength of purpose in sticking to the point. What then is the main-stream in this scene?

It lies, I think, in the utterances of Theseus and particularly where at first sight they seem discursive. There he stands, right at the beginning of the scene, warming his hands at the blaze, and letting his thoughts wander over the story that the lovers have told of their experiences—their midsummer night's dream. I don't believe it, he says: lovers

and madmen are like that, and—as an afterthought—poets
too: they imagine things. And he enlarges on the power of a
poet's imagination: Dover Wilson rather oddly refers to his
lines as "the glorious quip beginning 'the poet's eye in a fine
frenzy rolling.' " [1] Certainly there is a touch of genial satire
in his description of the Bunthorne-look, but there the jest
is suspended for a moment, while the Duke is carried away
by his own idea and gives the most searching analysis (more
than cool reason ever comprehends) of the poet's function:
judge when you hear:

> The Poets eye, in a fine frenzy rolling,
> Doth glance from heauen to earth, from earth to heauen.
> And as imagination bodies forth
> The formes of things vnknowne, the Poets penne
> Turnes them to fhapes, and giues to ayery nothing
> A locall habitation and a name. [2]

It is one of those moments, rare but recurring and always
unexpected, when Shakespeare speaks straight to his
audience almost forgetting his intermediary: the mood is
usually provoked by contemplation of his own art, whether
as poet or player. [3] The exalted strain sinks almost as soon as
it has risen, and Theseus is quite matter-of-fact in his next
statement, which may be paraphrased: "Imagination is so
resourceful that if it wants some delight or other, it immediately creates the means to get it." And then he returns, with
a deliberate comic bathos, to the subject under discussion,
the lovers' experience in the wood at night: "How eafie is a
bufh fuppof'd a Beare." The bathos, to which some critics
rather sadly object, is appropriate as giving us the Duke's
tolerant scepticism. He has been carried away from his

---

[1] M.N.D. (*New Cambridge Shakespeare*), p. 86.

[2] The irregular verse-lining and eccentric punctuation of the Quarto
are not here reproduced. No student of the play should overlook Dover
Wilson's masterly exposition of the reasons for the printer's irregularity.
For reference, see above, p. 93, note.

[3] Other familiar examples are to be found in *A.Y.L.I.*, II. vii. 139,
Macbeth, V. v. 19.

purpose of decrying the lovers' story by his rhapsody on the imagination, and must recover himself. Meanwhile our attention has been fixed by his impressive lines, and the impression persists.

With the arrival of the lovers, the trend of the scene's action becomes immediately clear:

> Come now: what maskes, what daunces fhall wee haue,
> To weare away this long age of three hours?

(the pretty irony of the antithesis!)

> Where is our vfuall manager of mirth?
> What Reuels are in hand?

The setting is pure Elizabethan. Philostrate is Master of the Revels, whose job was to choose plays to be acted at Court: the Chamberlain's Men must often have known the anxiety of an audition. We need not read any autobiography into the fact that Philostrate is painted as a sort of Malvolio, unable to suffer fools gladly. There must be rival entertainments for Theseus to exercise his choice: Shakespeare makes use of both apt Greek colour and topical contemporary allusion to give interest to the items. Then we hear of the "tedious briefe Scene" of *Pyramus and Thisby*, and Philostrate's assumption, "no, my noble Lord, it is not for you", confirms the Duke's determination to hear that play—

> For neuer any thing can be amiffe,
> When fimpleneffe and duety tender it.

While the actors are being summoned, Theseus and Shakespeare enter upon another excursion which is clearly intended to prepare the ground for the tongue-tied simplicity of Quince's prologue and the subsequent play. "Our fport fhall be," he says, "to take what they miftake"—in other words, it will be interesting to see if we can appreciate the points which the actors themselves are not clever enough to understand and make plain. Good advice, which would make many an indifferent performance of Shakespeare seem sport; and how often the poet does in fact survive mishandling! Theseus continues with a description of what to the judicious among his audience must have been a familiar episode in the Queen's royal progresses—the stage-fright of the "great Clerkes" who have practised their "premeditated welcomes". After his gentle mimicry of the confused official, he turns back to Hippolyta:

> Truſt me, ſweete,
> Out of this ſilence, yet, I pickt a welcome:
> And in the modeſty of fearefull duty,
> I read as much, as from the rattling tongue
> Of ſaucy and audacious eloquence.

Now whereto tends all this? Which side is Shakespeare on—the players or the audience? It is one of his greatest strengths as a dramatist that he will not take sides—who will tell us whether he is pro-Falstaff, or anti-Macbeth?—and here in this scene he holds the balance, with Theseus's help, as beautifully as ever. It is a singularly cunning stroke by which he has his own actors—the Duke and his Court—sitting with their backs to us on the front edge of the stage like the real gallants who pestered the actors with their impudent comments, and so both forestalls criticism and at the same time gives his audience a picture of themselves, holding a mirror up to nature and showing scorn her own image. And so nicely is the balance held that we cannot be certain—nor could the Globe audience either—just whither the satire is directed. Only it is clear that Theseus, although now and again he does not resist the temptation to make his jest, is at pains to give the actors a fair chance and to teach the company, his bride included, the courtesy of a cultured patron.

The audience then settle comfortably round the fire to watch the play beyond it. We, no less than the court, are now sitting about the hearth: we may make our comments too, if we will. The actor who plays Quince need have no

D

doubt as to how to speak his prologue: Shakespeare has just told him:

> I haue feene them fhiuer and looke pale,
> Make periods in the midft of fentences,
> Throttle their practiz'd accent in their feares,
> And in conclufion dumbly haue broke off,
> Not paying mee a welcome.

"All for your delight," says Quince, "wee are not here". When the trumpet blows for the second time, the inset curtain parts to reveal our old friends in all their new finery. During Quince's next speech they go through their whole drama at lightning speed in dumb-show. Shakespeare means us to laugh at the absurdity of the practice, which is hardly less ridiculous when it occurs in *Hamlet*. Quince then retires to the side of the stage with his prompt-book, and the play begins in earnest.

In earnest it must be. The mechanicals play their tragedy for all they are worth—only failing through their simplicity, their forgetfulness, their nervousness, their incompetence, or (most venial reason) their absent-minded admiration of Bottom's virtuosity. And all the time they are acutely conscious of the grandeur of the occasion, the distinction of their audience: woe betide the Bottom who forgets his place—except for that once when artistic integrity prompts him to put even the Duke right with his "No, in truth Sir, he fhould not." Too often when this scene is played, we carry away no impression of the meeting of young Pyramus and his love Thisby by moonlight, because the actors are too busy asking us to laugh at their superfluous horse-play. Certainly Shakespeare means Bottom and Flute to be absorbed in their parts, and if they play their tragedy with conviction, the comedy will take care of itself; it is their unconscious absurdity that makes us laugh. And after all what the mechanicals are trying to do is what, *mutatis mutandis*, Shakespeare and his fellows were constantly trying to do; to create an illusion with scant materials, to

make something out of nothing. Have we not just been
reminded of this? The truth is contained in the Duke's
phrase about the poet's pen that

> giues to ayery nothing
> A locall habitation and a name.

That phrase, that famous speech—a set-piece for the
anthologists—is after all not an irrelevant ornament: it is
well-placed where it stands, looking both forward and
back—back to the midnight magic of the wood, which is
entirely the creation of the poet's pen (how easy is a bush
supposed a bear!); and forward to the attempted illusion of
Pyramus and Thisby (how easy is a tinker supposed a wall!)
The point is made perfectly clear during the brief interval
at the end of "scene one", when Wall retires from the stage.
Theseus has risen to stretch his legs and warm his hands at
the fire; Hippolyta, still seated, says with the brutal blunt-
ness of the unimaginative philistine: "This is the filliest
stuffe, that euer I heard." Whereupon her lord rounds on
her (facing also the audience) and says with his former
impressiveness, "The best, in this kinde, are but shadowes:
and the worst are no worse, if imagination amend them."
There is a continuity of theme holding this scene together,
and Theseus is its spokesman. It is a theme that is naturally
often in Shakespeare's mind, but with tactful restraint he
does not let it occupy his stage too often: he does not make
the mistake of so many authors who suppose that they
themselves and their art are of absorbing interest to their
public: when he touches on his art, the expression of his own
pride in it and consciousness of its power is usually seasoned
with a phrase of affectionate contempt ("poore Player, That
struts and frets his houre vpon the Stage"); here all the
labours of the players are held up to ridicule, but we are not
allowed to forget that they are the amateurs of Shakespeare's
own profession by which the Chamberlain's Men—the best
in this kind—made their bread and butter.

The remedy, says Shakespeare through the mouth of Theseus, is to amend with the imagination.

> Such trickes hath ftrong imagination,
> That if it would but apprehend fome ioy,
> It comprehends fome bringer of that ioy.

It is after all the same tune as *Henry the Fifth* (a 1599 play): let us "on your imaginarie Forces worke . . . Peece out our imperfections with your thoughts . . . For 'tis your thoughts that now muft deck our Kings." It is no less ridiculous to say

> Suppofe within the Girdle of thefe Walls
> Are now confin'd two mightie Monarchies,
> Whofe high, up-reared, and abutting Fronts
> The perillous narrow Ocean parts afunder . . .

than

> This lome, this roughcaft, and this ftone doth fhowe
> That I am that fame wall: the truth is fo.

Peter Quince and William Shakespeare are at the same job, and Shakespeare does not mean us to miss the point. That is why Theseus says that the best in this kind are but shadows.

Meanwhile let us not at any price spoil the effect by putting Snout inside one of those painted canvas boxes so often made for him. Let him have some plaster, or some loam, or some rough-cast about him: a couple of sacks borrowed from an Athenian miller will make an excellent substructure. Your painted canvas would lead logically to a vista of moonlit fruit-trees for Capulet's orchard. No, no:

let imagination amend, prompted by the poet's pen. It is
indeed a sweet and lovely wall, without such meretricious aids.
Improvisation of property and costume is the glory of charades,
and the atmosphere of charades is what is wanted here.

One of the minor miracles of this miraculous play is the
text of Peter Quince's tragedy of *Pyramus and Thisby*. It is
unnecessary to point to each detail of Shakespeare's satire:
he aims his shaft at all the theatrical tricks in turn—prologue,
dumb-show, soliloquy, apostrophe, alliteration, rhetorical
repetition, they are all there, together with the absurdity of
rhyme-patterns and the staleness of poetical commonplace.
I suppose only one who can write so well as Shakespeare,
can write so ill on purpose; just as it takes the best of musicians to give the perfect burlesque of faulty intonation. It is
as well perhaps to remember that most of these artifices are
employed by Shakespeare himself in his first four acts
when he is as eager to create illusion as Quince himself.
Lysander and Hermia, Helena and Demetrius use the whole
box of tricks, without making a false move: a twist of the
screw, and Pyramus and Thisby are just that much out of
focus which makes nonsense of the whole picture. But the
actors must be wholly unaware of the absurdity, and I can
see Shakespeare's indignation, when a Tarlton or a Kempe—
and there have been many since his day—set on some
quantity of barren spectators to laugh, though in the mean-
time some necessary question of the play was then to be
considered. The Wall, taken unawares by Pyramus's question
may join in the search for Thisby, or even react to the swift
succession of compliments and curses: the Moon will
become impatient of interruption, as he gives a prose
summary of the speech he has learnt in verse and twice
begun: Pyramus will provoke laughter when he rises from
the floor at "Now am I dead": Thisby will never quite
adjust the realism of her pathos to the mechanical structure
of the verse in which it is expressed, and will no doubt cry
"Come trusty sword" before she has made sure of its where-
abouts, so that the dead hand of her lover must offer her the

means of destruction. But the actors will all throughout stick to the job in hand, which is the tragic story of Pyramus and Thisby; when things go wrong, it will be because of their enthusiastic inexperience—a defect which extends, of course, to the text of their play. If the clowns fulfil Shakespeare's intention, then there will be plenty of laughter—and also an added significance in the well-chosen words of the Duke's commendation: truly a fine tragedy, "and very notably difcharg'd."

The comments of the Duchess and the gallants are witless enough; and the Duke himself, though he has moments of insight, as I have suggested, and though his influence is used to restrain the interruptions, joins in the barracking with some frigid jests. No audience, busy laughing at the clowns, will spare much breath to respond to these superior sallies, and it is tempting to suppose that Shakespeare was aware of this and hoped that a certain section of his audience might notice it too and take it for what it was, a satirical comment on themselves. "You think we are like Bottom and Co., don't you?" he seems to say. "Do you know what *you* are like?" But of course as usual he does not take sides. He merely presents a picture of a play in progress, of the old game of make-believe, his own profession. Make-believe needs an audience: there must be someone to make believe, someone on whom the illusion is to be cast: so his picture contains an audience too, one member of which is almost enlightened; at least he says a thing or two which show him to be the kind of judicious person a poet likes to address—"the cenfure of which one, muft in your allowance ore-weigh a whole Theater of others."

THE Bergamask "between two of our company" may be just such an acrobatic clownish dance as the groundlings expected and Shakespeare probably abhorred: if so, the play will stand still at a point where it should be moving towards the shapely pattern of its end. But there is poetical force in the development of a hint of Shakespeare's in the scene of Bottom's waking.[1] Bottom has had a rare vision, in which presumably the salient features were his own Ass head and the Fairy Queen. With his usual resourcefulness he decides to get Quince to write a ballad of this dream, to sing in the latter end of the play before the Duke. "Peraduenture, to make it the more gratious, I ſhall ſing it at her death." At Thisby's death—that is the point we have now reached, and instead of the ballad we have a Bergamaſk, a clownish dance. Bottom and Flute therefore rise from their death to execute such a dance, Bottom wearing a paper Ass head and Flute, already clad in feminine garments, with a paper crown for the Fairy Queen. The tune is of course the Tongs-and-Bones. If it should be asked why the ballad became a dance, one may guess perhaps that it was Quince who objected: Bottom's reasonable good ear in music was not good enough for high society.

Aɴᴅ so while Philostrate is handing Bottom, if not sixpence a day, at least sixpence, the Court rises and our play is done.

The iron tongue of midnight hath tolde twelue.
Louers to bed—

---

[1] See above, p. 92.

But no, all is not done. Theseus with a chance word reminds us of what Shakespeare has been at pains to make us forget—

> tis almoſt Fairy time.

Being a sceptic, he speaks the words with playful irony: the irony rebounds pleasantly upon the speaker, for all unaware he tells the truth. The three couples go in graceful procession up the stair, the candles in the great hall are snuffed.[1]

With the candles out, the log-fire glows still in the centre of the platform. Out of the embers (through his favourite trap-door) rises Puck intent on curdling the blood a little— Puck the Goblin feared in field and town.

> Now the waſted brands doe glowe,
> Whilſt the ſcriech-owle, ſcrieching lowd,
> Puts the wretch, that lyes in woe,
> In remembrance of a ſhrowde.

Why this grisly note? and the howling wolf, and the ghosts that glide in the churchway paths? It is Quiller-Couch again who, in his introduction to the New Cambridge Edition, makes the answer plain. He sets this passage of Puck's side by side with a stanza from Spenser's *Epithalamion*, and asks: "Can anyone . . . doubt *A Midsummer Night's Dream* to be intended for a merry κάθαρσις, a pretty purgation, of those same goblin terrors which Spenser would exorcise from the bridal chamber?"[2] In fact, Oberon and Titania are coming to conduct a ceremonial purgation of the bridal house—the whole thing scaled down, of course, as before to fairy stature—and if this ceremony is to be dramatized, we must have some representation of the dangers to which the newly-wed couples are subject. Who can provide this if not Puck? And having thrown—oh so delicately—this shadow

---

[1] Quiller-Couch, in his *Cambridge Lectures* (J. M. Dent & Sons' Every-man edition), p. 140, suggests that the players made use sometimes of the dusk at the end of the afternoon for a lighting effect.

[2] *Loc. cit.*, pp. x.-xi.

across the candle-light of the happy lovers, he begins at once
to dispel the fear he has caused:

> And wee Fairies, that doe runne,
> By the triple Hecates teame,
> From the prefence of the Sunne,
> Following darkeneffe like a dreame,
> Now are frollick: not a moufe
> Shall difturbe this hallowed houfe.
> I am fent, with broome, before,
> To fweepe the duft, behinde the dore.

Already an advance-guard pokes his head round the
corner of a pillar, scouting to see if the coast is clear. Then
swiftly and stealthily they all come tripping in, all those
choir-boys who have waited so long for their cue, all with
strict instructions to be cherubs this time. Oberon and
Titania stand in the glow of the fire—

> Through the houfe giue glimmering light,
> By the dead and drowfie fier—

Each pair in turn, two to
a couplet, they light their
tapers in the glowing ashes.
Then as the song begins,
their tapers held aloft with
the mysterious gesture of
ritual, they purge the air of
the great chamber:

> Now, vntill the breake of
>   day,
> Through this houfe, each
>   Fairy ftray.
> To the beft bride bed will
>   wee:
> Which by vs fhall bleffed be:
> And the iffue, there create,
> Euer fhall be fortunate:

So ſhall all the couples three
Euer true in louing be:
And the blots of natures hand
Shall not in their iſſue ſtand.

Neuer mole, hare-lippe, nor ſcarre,
Nor marke prodigious, ſuch as are
Deſpiſed in natiuitie,
Shall vpon their children be.

Lastly, Puck at Oberon's bidding offers them a bowl of field-dew into which each in turn dips his hand:

With this field deaw confecrate,
Euery Fairy take his gate,
And each ſeuerall chamber bleſſe,
Through this palace, with ſweete peace,
And the owner of it bleſt
Euer ſhall in ſafety reſt.

The King gives the signal for departure—

>   Trippe away: make no ſtay:
>   Meete me all, by breake of day—

and they follow the lovers up the great staircase. As the
inset curtain pulls on a vision of Titania and Oberon
mounting the distant stair, Puck—the odd man out—dis-
appears back into the fire. His epilogue is no part of the
play: he speaks as an actor, the illusion gone; actors—and
their audience too, it seems—like this custom of dropping
the mask in public.

THERE is, I hope, not much novelty in this account of
the play: it attempts rather to strip away innovation,
to rediscover Shakespeare's purpose; and where the
evidence is less plain, to guess from Shakespeare's hints and
from what we gather in other plays of his tastes and inclina-

tions. For the gist of the matter is this: Shakespeare knew what he was about all the time, his stagecraft is masterly. Recapture the essential conditions of his theatre, and then follow his instructions: the instructions are most of them there, stated or implied, in the text of the play, and the search, if not easy, is an absorbing one. Each actor must know his place in the scheme, and Shakespeare's intention every time he sends him on to the stage. If you depart from the conditions and his instructions, you will fall into difficulties at once; and to get round those difficulties, you will seek irrelevant distractions—irrelevant scenery and effects, irrelevant eccentricities of costume, irrelevant clowning and "business", irrelevant music and spectacle; and you will end by cutting the text or gabbling the long speeches as if they were something to be ashamed of.

Shakespeare knew what he was about: he was an actor as well as a poet, and he found out the secret of poetic drama; which we have forgotten since.

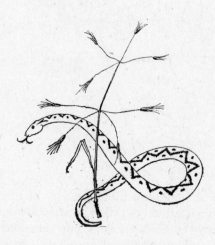

A Midſommer nights dreame.

As it hath beene ſundry times publickely acted, by the *Right honoura-*
ble, the Lord Chamberlaine his
ſeruants.

Written by William Shakeſpeare.

¶ Imprinted t London, for *Thomas Fiſher,* and are to
be ſoulde at is ſhoppe, at the Signe of the White Hart,
in *Fleeteſtreete.* 1600.

APPENDIX

★

THE production of *A Midsummer Night's Dream* in Harrow School Speech Room in July, 1945, was the fourth of a series of progressive experiments in recapturing the lost dramatic art of Shakespeare. In October, 1940, an incendiary bomb put the fore-curtain and floodlights out of action, and would-be Harrovian actors were confronted with something like the conditions of the Elizabethan theatre.

Twelfth Night (1941) was the tentative beginning: a cask rolled to the middle of the stage, a lamp swinging in Sir Toby's unsteady hand, and faith, sir, we were carousing till the second cock. Much was learnt about the stagecraft of the play, and—most important lesson of all—that Shakespeare had himself anticipated every difficulty, and solved most of them quite simply thus: "What Country (Friends) is this?" "This is Illyria Ladie."—"Not to bee a bedde after midnight, is to be vp betimes."—"This is the ayre, that is the glorious Sunne." *Henry the Fifth* (1942) was a much more formidable problem, as Shakespeare was well aware in 1599. Bending up every spirit to his full height, he produced a solution in the words of the Chorus, whereby we crossed the Channel, stormed Harfleur, and—in the steady daylight of Speech Room—camped in the expectant night before Agincourt. How truly dark that night was, a chance conversation at next year's rehearsal revealed. In 1943 it was to be *Macbeth*, and Banquo's murderer was dismayed to hear that he would have to cut his victim's throat in broad daylight. When he was told that it would be just like the scene in the camp on the night before Agincourt, "Oh yes," he answered, still unconvinced, "but then it *was* dark." By the time *Macbeth* reached performance, even ghosts and apparitions were not afraid to face the daylight of Speech Room.

In 1944 the flying bombs interrupted this annual series of experiments. *The Merchant of Venice* was abandoned a fortnight before production. But the next year, with peace in Europe, it was possible to present *A Midsummer Night's Dream*, and the attempt was made to reproduce one of the performances of the play in 1599 at the Globe, "as it hath beene sundry times publickely acted, by the Right honourable, the Lord Chamberlaine his servants." The actor who spoke the part of the Chorus in *Henry the Fifth* was dressed as Shakespeare himself. Shakespeare returned in person in 1945 to deliver a prologue written for the occasion and addressed to his constant audience. Three paragraphs from this prologue will give some idea of the scope and purpose of these experiments:

> *Gentles and friends, who climb this ancient Hill,*
> *Pray welcome Shakespeare as your author still.*
> *Three years of war, three years of grief and danger,*
> *You had the heart to entertain a stranger—*
> *Yet not a stranger, sure, to you who can*
> *Proclaim that you began when I began.*
>
> *Here in this room, in nineteen forty-one,*
> *For the first time your miracle was done.*
> *You told yourselves that what my plays most needed*
> *Was simply to present them just as we did—*
> *No curtain here in front, no darkened hall,*
> *No scenery, no lights, nothing at all.*
> *Three times you proved, in every play you heard,*
> *My sharpest weapon is the spoken word.*
> *You saw Olivia's garden by this spell,*
> *Sir Toby's cellar and Malvolio's cell;*
> *Harfleur was sieged and taken in this room,*
> *The eve of Agincourt spread here its gloom;*
> *Words made the midnight of King Duncan slain*
> *And brought tall Birnam wood to Dunsinane.*
> *In such a night Lorenzo was to woo*
> *Last year the pretty daughter of the Jew;*
> *But that the bombast of the flying menace*
> *Shook the foundations of Belmont and Venice.*
>
> *Now once again I view this well-loved scene—*
> *How like a winter hath my absence been!—*
> *See with new joy this noble scaffoldage—*
> *Burbage himself would know this for a stage;*
> *And on this day of blest reunion, I*
> *Bring you my old enchanted comedy,*
> *Ask you to dream away two summer hours—*
> *Titania's dream? or Bottom's? mine, or yours?*
> *No matter—if you let a poet's spell*

Work its own magic charm, all will be well.
Forget this summer's day that this is Speecher:
Let me transform you each familiar feature,
The pillars pine-trees and the arching roof
Haunted with owls, webbed with the spider's woof;
Here in this daylight let the moon prevail
And cast deep shadows over hill and dale.
Such tricks imagination comprehends;
Listen to Theseus, as this evening ends.

The "noble scaffoldage"—first used in 1945—was an attempt to reproduce the dimensions of the Globe stage as described by John Cranford Adams. The ground-plan of Speech Room, about 80 feet across, is much the same size—though not the same shape—as the Globe, and it was found possible by bridging the well of Speech Room, to place the main acting arena right forward in the midst of the audience. For those who would like to test and prove the astonishing gain of such an arrangement, the plan here sketched on the lines of Cranford Adams's diagram[1] gives the essentials. The relative proportion of platform and audience, and the position of the platform *in the midst of the audience*, are more important than the actual dimensions.

When the inset-curtains are closed, there are three main entries to the stage—R stage-door, L stage-door, and Centre through the curtain. When the curtains are open, there are two more—R inset and L inset. Also on the main stage there is an entry through the Trap. If there is no Trap available, Puck will have to make other shift for himself.

Essential, too, is the daylight of afternoon at the Globe. If the production is indoors, it may be necessary to reinforce with artificial light. But it must be a steady light, representing the Elizabethan afternoon, with no attempt to dim for moonlight or tinge with red for dawn: what we start with we must go on with, except in so far as candles and tapers can give an effect of brilliance to the last scene.

Apart from the Trap-door, these essential conditions are not difficult to realize in any hall of ordinary dimensions: it will probably mean abandoning the usual platform, and marking out the stage on the floor of the hall. The gain in intimate contact

---

[1] *The Globe Playhouse*, p. 53. See also the diagram on p. 20, above.

with the audience will more than compensate for the loss of
seating space.

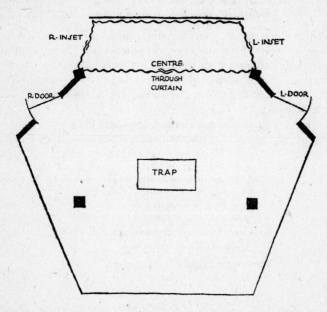

The following notes, based on the Harrow production, may
perhaps be of use to acting companies, whether professional or
amateur, who wish to examine by practical test the belief that
the best way to realize Shakespeare's plays is the way in which
he saw them himself.

Shakespeare's 1945 prologue, quoted above, ends with a special
plea for a fair hearing for the music:

> *Before we start, I ask your leave to say*
> *One word about the music to our play.*
> *Lend us your ears; and if you never heard*
> *Of my good friends, Tom Weelkes and William Byrd,*
> *Nor know that England's song was once her pride,*
> *And beat the jigging foreigner beside,*
> *Give ear to what your countrymen can do—*
> *If England to herself remain but true!—*
> *To-day the music is to listen to.*

E

Strike up, musicians, with a cheerful ring;
ALL CREATURES NOW ARE MERRY MINDED, *sing.*
Awake the pert and nimble spirit of mirth
And celebrate sweet peace returned to earth.

While Shakespeare, carrying the prompt-book, takes his seat in the front row of the audience, the singers in a gallery aloft and out of sight strike up with John Bennet's madrigal from Morley's collection, *The Triumphs of Oriana* (1601). The words of the madrigal, which is published separately by Stainer & Bell, Ltd., are as follows:

All creatures now are merry, merry-minded.
The shepherd's daughters playing,
The nymphs are fa-la-laing,
Yond bugle was well winded.
At Oriana's presence each thing smileth.
The flowers themselves discover:
Birds over her do hover:
Music the time beguileth.
See where she comes with flowery garlands crowned,
Queen of all queens renowned.

Then sang the shepherds and nymphs of Diana;
Long live fair Oriana.

Act One, Scene One

The first figure to appear on the stage (through curtain, Centre) is Philostrate, as the Duke's major-domo, a sort of Malvolio in this Elizabethan household. He summons the attendants (R and L doors): let them be lively, if not individual, modelled on Capulet's servants: their function to strew more rushes on the already strewn stage: four is about as many as the Chamberlain's Men can afford: add two pages, whose untidy dress comes under the disapproving eye of Philostrate. At a given moment, marked in the music by the phrase "*See where she comes,*" the major-domo calls them to attention, the pages part the centre curtain, and Theseus and Hippolyta appear to the loyal strains of

Long live fair Oriana.

15   Exit Philostrate, by R door.
20   Enter Egeus, etc., by L door.

The grouping of this full scene is worth recording here in

diagram, since it typifies at once the three-dimensional quality
of the Globe stage as opposed to the pictorial flatness of the
modern box-stage. Hermia, who is at the moment the centre of
interest, is almost central facing down-stage: Theseus, the arbiter,
is one side of her, Egeus, the plaintiff, on the other: the rival
suitors, called forth in turn by Egeus, stand down-stage, making
literally—as they also do metaphorically—a triangle with apex
Hermia. Their backs are turned on most of the audience: but on
this stage there is little or no danger of "masking": wherever

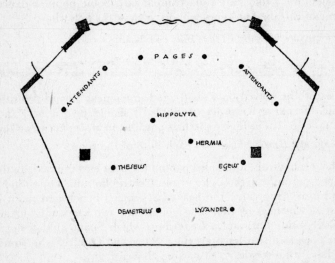

you may be in the audience, you feel yourself not to be watching
a distant picture but to be standing as an interested spectator on
the edge of the central group. Like you, the attendants stand on
the edge of the group: Hippolyta is nearer the centre of things,
but she too is aloof, until at l. 113, and more definitely at l. 122,
Theseus is at pains to bring her into the picture.

127　Exeunt all but Lysander and Hermia. Long processional
　　　exit by R door: covered by the cadence of Bennet's madrigal
　　from "*Then sang the shepherds* . . ."
179　Enter Helena, by L door: she makes at a run for R door,
　　　but is checked in mid-stage by Hermia's greeting.
224　Exit Hermia, by L door.

225   Exit Lysander, by R door.

225–251   The formal part of Helena's soliloquy down-stage
          centre, to give intimate contact with the audience. At
I will goe tell him . . . a hurried movement towards the L door,
through which she goes after the final couplet.

Act One, Scene Two

As soon as Helena is gone, strike up the tune "Tongs-and-
Bones" on a solo flute (unaccompanied). Some popular dance-
tune of Elizabethan times will do, such as the following:

(From Giles Farnaby's *Tower Hill*, a keyboard piece):

Tune: to be played on a shrill wind instrument (Penny Whistle,
Fife, Piccolo or Recorder; if visible, it should be " à bec," not
" traverso") at as high a pitch as possible, in any convenient key.

Tongs and Bones: bang with each note of the tune.

The mechanicals, assembled behind the inset curtain, take up the
tune, and appear through curtain Centre. Bottom, Flute, Snout
and Starveling carry the heavy carpenter's bench and plant it
just down-stage of the Trap: on it are two tarpaulins folded
neatly inside out, and a tree-stump which Snout lifts off on to
the floor as a seat for Starveling. Snug and Quince, who comes
in last, bring trestles to sit on (see above, p. 25).

15   *Masters, spread yourselves.* All except Bottom, who roams free
     about the stage, sit round or on the bench for their com-
mittee. Starveling plies his trade with needle and scissors on a
hem of the tarpaulin (see above, p. 25).

58   Starveling, hearing that he is to play *Thysbyes mother*, may
     drape his shoulders in one end of a tarpaulin.

72   Then, at Quince's *fright the Dutchesse*, Starveling will
     imitate the scared ladies and by his frightened run unfold
his tarpaulin to its full extent.

85   *Well: I will undertake it.* There has been anxious suspense
     over Bottom's sulks: when he agrees to play the part, there
is a general sigh of relief, and during the discussion between him

and Quince on the colour of beards, the rest may complete the
unfolding of the tarpaulins, and rig them over bench and trestles.
The tree-stump must also be put in position (see above, p. 25).

106 *Enough: holde, or cut bowſtrings.* The mechanicals retire as
they came, through the Centre of the curtain, humming
the tune of Tongs-and-Bones, and leaving in the middle of the
stage a puzzle for the audience to interpret.

Act Two, Scene One

They are not left long to ponder. This is the critical moment
for make-believe. Nothing but Shakespeare's own reckless
assurance will do to pull it off. Here are the bald facts.

At a convenient cadence of the Tongs-and-Bones, the singers
aloft in the gallery break in with Weelkes' five-part ballet *On the
plains* (published by Stainer & Bell, Ltd.). The whole, without
repeats, is not too long for the purpose: the words, by Barnabe
Barnes, are as follows:

> *On the plains*
> *Fairy trains*
> *Were a-treading measures:*
> *Satyrs played,*
> *Fairies stayed,*
> *At the stops set leisures.*
> *Fa la.*
>
> *Nymphs begin*
> *To come in,*
> *Quickly, thick and threefold:*
> *Now they dance,*
> *Now they prance,*
> *Present there to behold.*
> *Fa la.*

Choosing the moment so that the dialogue can begin as soon
as the music ends (*Nymphs begin To come in* is dramatically suitable), "*Enter a Fairie at one doore*"—R stage door. There is no
clear indication in the text whether this Fairy is male or female:
but from the nature of her duties, and for the dramatic appropriateness of a contrast between Titania's servant and Oberon's
Puck, I suppose it to be one of the Ladies of the Queen's Bedchamber. Her immediate business is to deck the tarpaulin-clad
bench with flowers and foliage, and she is just hurrying off on

further errands of the same kind for the Queen, *to dew her orbs vpon the greene . . . and hang a pearle in euery couſlippes eare,* when she is checked by the urgent whisper of Puck, *How now ſpirit, whither wander you?* Puck has bobbed up from the trap-door on to the top of the bench, taking both her and the audience by surprise. The bench has already become a flower-strewn bank.

7   Let her look up at *the Moons ſphere;* Puck too, following her gesture. We have been prepared long ago for this moon by Shakespeare (see above, p. 27 and note).

60   "*Enter the King of Fairies, at one doore, with his traine; and the Queene, at another, with hers.*" The assured simplicity of Shakespeare's stagecraft speaks vividly through this direction. To make clear the point that the Fairies are imitating the Elizabethan mortals in costume and manners, let this entry recall at once the opening entry of Theseus and Hippolyta: let some of the attendant fairies strew rushes, even in the wood! Titania's train picks itself: the Lady of the Bedchamber will need one colleague: then there are four gentlemen, Peaseblossom, Cobweb, Moth and Mustardseed. Oberon will therefore need half a dozen henchmen to balance these; and Puck his jester, to upset the balance. How many choir-boys the Chamberlain's Men could count on, I cannot tell: but the stretched resources of the wardrobe would set a limit. King, Queen, jester and a round dozen of others would amply fill the "groue or greene." I doubt if Mark Antony was allowed many morè to sway with his oratory.

Music to give "more grace to their action": the "fa la's" from *On the plains.*

63   *Tarry, raſh wanton.* Titania, at the unexpected and unwelcome sight of Oberon, motions to her train to retreat by the L door, from which they have just come. The King's discourteous command checks their flight, and the Queen, before replying, mounts the flower-strewn bank. From this position she dominates the scene during her eloquent defiance.

145   "Fa la's" from *On the plains* to cover exit of Titania and her train by L door.

147   . . . *torment thee, for this iniury.* Oberon motions his train off by R door. Both trains, especially Oberon's, show signs of being "off parade," as they go (see above, p. 68).

176   Puck starts his journey round about the earth by plunging
      into the Trap.

187   Oberon retires up against the inset curtain. If the King of
      Fairies says *I am inuiſible*, we must of course believe him.

Demetrius and Helena enter by L door. Demetrius (like
Lysander later) will wear his boots to show he is out of doors:
and it is up to the actors, with the help of Shakespeare's words,
to persuade us that they are in a wood at night, at *the mercy of
wilde beaſtes.*

230 ff. The dove pursues the griffin round the obstacle of the
         bank. No doubt the Chamberlain's Men found the pillars
supporting the canopy of the "heavens" useful to help Demetrius
give Helena the slip.

242–244   Both Demetrius and Helena go out by R door.

246   Puck returns through Trap.

268   Exit Oberon L door, Puck R door.

Act Two, Scene Two

The singers break in on Puck's line with "*Nymphs begin To
come in . . .*" from *On the plains.* The inset curtain is drawn for the
first time in the play, disclosing on the left Titania's couch, just
described by Oberon; and on the right, the hawthorn-brake,
tiring-house for the mechanicals (see above, pp. 28-29). The
opening of the inset gives great extra depth to the stage, and
with its suggestion of trees makes the audience feel as if it were
in a clearing with dense forest all round.

One particular crisis in the building of the Harrow production
is worth dwelling on, as showing how hard it is to learn the
elementary lesson. In Speech Room it was necessary to absorb
two structural pillars in the inset space: these inevitably formed
the nucleus of Titania's couch and the hawthorn-brake. The first
design entailed masking the exposed parts of the two pillars in
bark: the process proved difficult and laborious, and when it
was complete, the result did not look right. Once again recourse

to the Chamberlain's Men provided the solution. They had no pillars in their inset: but they had two supporting the "heavens" right out on the fore-stage itself, exposed to view ever since the beginning of the play. The practised eye of their audience was used to thinking of them as a maypole, a notice-board, a roadside cross—what you will, according to the author's prompting[1]: and when in the moonlit wood Helena chased Demetrius, he dodged her round—a tree, of course. Bark was a self-conscious affectation of reality. The device was abandoned: the bare pillars bore leafy branches and, for all their gleaming surface, were accepted without question by the audience as the trunks of trees. The new freedom of make-believe seemed to have the blessing of Shakespeare himself.

We now have three pieces of stage furniture—the word is more appropriate than scenery. We will call them for brevity the Couch and the Brake in the inset, and the Bank on the fore-stage. Each of the three has its practical purpose in the evolution of the play, as will appear in the following notes.

1   *Come, now a Roundell and a Fairy ſong.* The Queen and her six attendants enter from R inset. She speaks her first line during the music, and the roundel is danced by Peaseblossom (the soldier) and Mustardseed (the Spanish courtier) with the two Ladies of the Bedchamber, to the accompaniment of the "Fa la's."

2-8   The offices may be distributed among the gentlemen— Moth unsheathing a dagger to kill cankers, Peaseblossom sharpening his sword to deal with the reremice, and Mustardseed drawing a long bow at the clamorous owl. Cobweb meanwhile will preside at the head of the Couch.

9-26   Distribution as follows: 9, 10, Peaseblossom; 11, 12, Moth; 13, 14, a Lady invoking the nightingale to sing. Only the refrain is sung, by the hidden singers: the music is from William Byrd's *Lullaby, my sweet little Baby*, adapted for this secular purpose by Hector McCurrach:

---

[1] Cf. J. Cranford Adams, *The Globe Playhouse*, p. 112.

(Byrd's Lullaby is published by Stainer & Bell, Ltd.).

Then 20, 21, Mustardseed; 22, 23, Cobweb; 24, 25, a Lady as

before; and the refrain by the singers. The fairies on the stage may appear to be singing the Lullaby.

All through this passage the Ladies of the Bedchamber have been composing Titania to sleep. As the Lullaby ends, one of the Ladies springs forward from the bedside and, with an urgent whisper, says *Hence away: now all is well: One aloofe, ſtand Centinell.*

26   Peaseblossom is the sentinel: as he paces up and down his beat, the singers repeat a brief phrase of the cadence. Oberon appears from L inset, behind the Couch, and motions to three of his henchmen who appear like conspirators, R inset, from behind the Brake, and as the Lullaby ends for the last time, overpower and gag Peaseblossom and carrying him struggling off stage, R inset. Let this be an act of war—no prettiness about these fairies. The Queen is at the King's mercy.

34   Exit Oberon, L inset. Titania remains sleeping in full view: it is strange how easily we shall forget her presence, until Shakespeare reminds us.

35   Enter Lysander and Hermia, R door.

40   *vpon this banke* . . . This is of course the fore-stage Bank, which must, as appears from this passage, be big enough for Lysander to *ly further off.* The demand for sleeping accommodation in this play is so great that it looks as if some such device as the draped carpenter's bench was an essential part of the mechanism of the Chamberlain's Men's production.

65   Hermia sleeps at the left end of the Bank, Lysander at the right end.

66   Puck enters by the R door, and wearily mounts the Bank, whence peering over he catches sight of the lovers in turn.

83   Exit Puck, L door. Demetrius and Helena run in by R door.

87   Demetrius runs out by L door.

100   Helena advancing R of the Bank, catches sight of Lysander.

134   Exit Helena, R door.

144   Lysander follows Helena through R door.

145–156   Hermia's soliloquy is an opportunity to reinforce the idea of the terrors of loneliness in the wood at night. She runs out by L door.

Act Three, Scene One

Straight on, with no musical join. Distant hallooing and whistling behind R door. Quince enters first, peering with a lantern, selects *this greene plot*—the space between the Bank and the inset—for his stage, and decides that *this hauthorne brake* will do for the tiring-house. Then he whistles for the others. He sets his lantern and prompt-book on the right end of the Bank, from which point of vantage, with his back half-turned to Titania's Couch, he will rehearse the play in front of the Brake.

75 *What hempen homeſpunnes . . .* Puck springs up through the Trap and sits on the Bank, behind Quince's back, to watch the play.

85 Exit Bottom behind the Brake, R inset.

86 Puck, bent on mischief, dodges down into the Trap.

100 Puck reappears on the Bank from the Trap, beckoning on the translated Bottom, who enters with the Ass head from the Brake. The grouping at this point is best represented by a diagram:

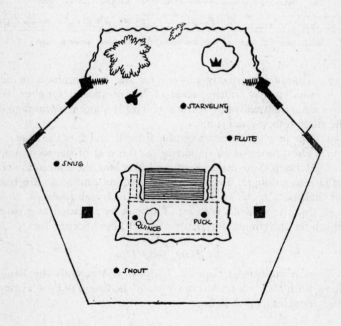

103 *Pray masters fly masters:* Snug runs out of R door, Flute
      L door; Quince takes temporary refuge in the Trap, and
Snout in front of the Bank, where he is hidden from Bottom;
Starveling, being deaf, is the last to become aware of trouble,
but roused to consciousness by the Ass's muzzle over his shoulder,
runs out L inset.

109 Puck, after chasing each in turn, vanishes L inset.

112–115 Snout trying to escape the monster, dodges out L door.

116 Quince popping up from the Trap, runs off by R door.

123 The tune, if Bottom can manage it, is the Tongs-and-Bones.

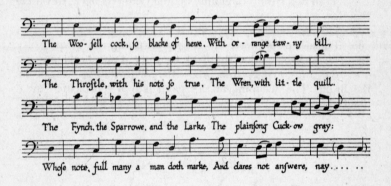

The Woo-sell cock, so blacke of hewe, With or-range taw-ny bill,

The Throstle, with his note so true, The Wren, with lit-tle quill.

The Fynch, the Sparrowe, and the Larke, The plainsong Cuck-ow gray:

Whose note, full many a man doth marke, And dares not answere, nay . . . .

127 Titania is perfectly placed, for the full emphasis of her
      waking: yet, during most of her prolonged slumber, we
have been unaware of her presence. This is another advantage of
the three-dimensional stage.

159 The four gentlemen assemble from R and L of the inset.

199 The procession of departure at the end of the scene goes
      R inset. New music is wanted here, for the romantic vein
of Titania's dotage. Suitable both for sound and sense are bars
51 (half-bar) to 58 of John Wilbye's madrigal *Draw on, sweet
night* (Stainer & Bell's edition). This can be repeated at greater
length for the companion picture of Act Four, Scene One.

Act Three, Scene Two

Oberon appears at once by L door, and ascends the Bank:
there, with his back turned down-stage, he listens to Puck's story.

4 Puck enters by R door.

7 ff.   He re-enacts the scene we have just witnessed, acting all
        the parts—Pyramus, Thisby, the panic-stricken mechani-
cals, and at last Titania—in the very positions where we have
just seen them. He even throws in a sketch of the creeping fowler
and the cawing choughs of his imagination: such is the virtue of
the unlocalized stage (see above, pp. 80 ff.).

41   Oberon and Puck retire to the inset, where they watch,
        half-hidden by the leaves of the Brake. Hermia and
Demetrius enter by L door.

81   Exit Hermia, by R door.

87   Demetrius sleeps in front of the Bank. Oberon and Puck
        come forward.

101   Puck's swift departure is by R door. Oberon stoops over
        Demetrius's recumbent head, as he speaks his incantation.

110   Puck returns by R door.

121   King and jester retire as before to the screen of the Brake.
        Lysander and Helena enter by R door.

137   Helena is of course down-stage, so that she is the first thing
        that Demetrius sees on waking.

177   Hermia's entry is also by R door.

    The whole of the vast stage is now at the disposal of this lively
quartet for their tempestuous quarrel. Not much movement is
invited by the lyrical pathos of Helena's long speeches. But from
Lysander's *Stay, gentle Helena* . . . (245) all restraint is thrown to
the winds: the swift thrust and parry of the dialogue is well
matched by swift chase, retreat and counter-attack across the
breadth and depth of the stage: in this scene the boy-actors, too,
will be in their element.

338   Lysander and Demetrius go, *cheeke by iowle*, R inset.

344   Hermia chases Helena off L inset.

345–395   The dialogue between Oberon and Puck, apart from
            its furthering of the plot, has two important purposes
to fulfil in atmospheric scene-painting; first, to prepare us for
the immediate fog, to be induced by Puck with his macabre
incantation *vp & down* . . .; secondly, to hint at the coming dawn,
the end of the midsummer night.

395   Exit Oberon, L inset.

400   *Here comes one.* Puck hides behind Titania's Couch, and
        imitates Demetrius's voice from there. Enter Lysander, by
R door.

404 Exit Lysander, by L door. Puck crosses in inset to hide in
     Brake. Enter Demetrius, by R door.

412 Puck's will-o-the-wisp voice trails off in R inset. Demetrius,
     who has circled the Bank in his pursuit, goes off where he
     came in, by R door. Re-enter Lysander, by L door.

420 Lysander lies down to sleep under the Brake, R inset. Puck
     leads Demetrius on again by R door.

425 Puck's *Come hither* spoken behind Titania's Couch, L inset.
     Demetrius chases the voice round the Couch, then gives
     up the chase.

430 Demetrius sleeps on the Couch. Enter Helena, by R door.

436 Helena sleeps on the Couch beside Demetrius. Puck appears
     in the inset between the three.

442 Hermia enters by L door.

447 She sleeps beneath the Brake, next to Lysander.

448 ff. Puck squeezes the juice on Lysander's eyes: then
         advances out of the inset for his dancing doggerel: at
the end he plunges into the Trap.

Here, though there is no dramatic need for one (see above,
p. 31), is an appropriate place for an Interval. With the
arrangement sketched above, it is possible to pull the inset
curtain and conceal the sleeping lovers from sight. The "Fa la's"
from *On the plains* may be sung to give more grace to the pulling
of the curtain.

Act Four, Scene One

When the audience are composed once more, the inset curtain
is gently pulled again, disclosing the four sleeping lovers, and
Oberon in the background watching invisible. At the same time
the musicians sing the music for Titania's dotage (as at the end
of III. i.): this time bars 51 (half-bar) to 68 of Wilbye's madrigal
fit well. Titania enters first from L door, with her Ladies in
attendance, and ushered in by Cobweb and Moth: Cobweb
gives his benediction to her new couch, the fore-stage Bank. At
an appropriate bass lead in the music (bar 62), Peaseblossom
and Mustardseed draw in Bottom (also by L door) and drag him
to the Queen's side. The immortal group of the Queen and her
monstrous lover, since the inset is already full, will therefore be
in front of the fore-stage Bank, a position which will give it all
the central emphasis it deserves.

5   *Where's Peaſe-bloſſome?* In this and the following lines, it is
     difficult to resist the temptation to transpose the names of
Peaseblossom and Cobweb. Peaseblossom, the soldier, seems the
right adventurer to send against the humble-bee; and Cobweb
better suited with the task of scratching. Shakespeare himself, by
an unexplained oversight, seems to concede this latter point
in l. 22.

29   No attempt is made to satisfy Bottom's desire for the
Tongs-and-Bones. The subject of music is tactfully shelved for
that of food.

41   *Faieries, be gon, and be alwaies away.* "All ways" (Theobald).
     Interpret Titania literally, and use every exit, including
     the Trap.

45   *How I dote on thee!* The same bars from *Draw on, sweet night,*
     accompany her doting slumber, while Puck creeps out of
the Trap, and Oberon advances from the inset.

83   *Muſick: ſuch as charmeth ſleepe.* This must not be the music
     of dotage, for the spell is broken: rather a phrase from the
Byrd Lullaby of II. ii. During the music, Puck gently detaches the
Ass head, and after his next line, contrives to drop it into the Trap.

85   *Sound Muſick:* Oberon's command produces a different
     music—the familiar "Fa la's" from *On the plains,* to which
King and Queen take hands and "rocke the ground" with their
dance.

102 Oberon and Titania trip after night's shade, R inset, to
     the accompaniment of "Fa la's." Puck is left alone for a
moment. The cadence of *On the plains* is interrupted by a "hunting
horn" in the distance L. Puck, startled out of his wits, scuttles
into the Trap. Immediately the singers break into their opening
madrigal: "*All creatures now are merry, merry-minded.*" Just before
their line "*Yond bugle was well winded,*" the "horn" sounds again
and nearer, in the same key, thus:

At "*See where she comes . . .*" the hunting-party begins to appear by L door; the four attendants, booted and with spears and bows; the two pages carrying a wicker hamper containing cups and a jug for the stirrup-cup (this they will set down on the fore-stage Bank, which becomes a sort of natural table for this scene, and has already lost its woodland quality of the previous night); Philostrate presiding fussily over the picnic arrangements; the Duke leading on the Duchess, who in a smart riding-habit is once again the cynosure of every eye; Egeus last, a somewhat reluctant follower of the hunt. The suggested stirrup-cup is a mere hint of the elaborate ritual of the Assembly before the Hunt, described in Turberville's *Booke of Hunting* (1576).[1] The touches suggested above, together with the horns and—chief factor—Shakespeare's words, will quickly conjure up an early-morning scene familiar to an Elizabethan audience and exhilarating to the spirits in any age.

111   *Difpatch I fay* . . . An attendant goes out by R door.

127   *But foft. What nymphes are thefe?* Egeus is first to notice the sleeping lovers, and he draws the Duke's attention to them.

138   Another attendant signals through R door. The horn sounds behind the door. The lovers start up and come forward on to the main stage.

186   To cover the departure of the Duke and Duchess and their train by L door, let the musicians sing as much of *All creatures now* . . . as is necessary for Philostrate to have the hamper decorously removed.

199   The lovers skip off by L door: no music; for their mood is delightfully informal.

The stage is apparently empty. But here once again the deep three-dimensional arena shows its resources. Bottom stretching and yawning will startle us; for he has been hidden all this time under our very noses—in front of the fore-stage Bank.

218   Bottom trots off to Athens by L inset, and the inset curtain is drawn on his departure. This is the cue for frenzied activity on the part of the stage hands, who have hitherto had a very easy time. They have to dismantle the Couch and the Brake, and set the palace stair, before V. i. 125. Their first task is to make room behind the curtain for the fore-stage Bank,

---

[1] Quoted with illustration in Marjorie and C. H. B. Quennell's *A History of Everyday Things in England*, Vol. 2, pp. 62-4.

which will be carried off as a carpenter's bench by the mechanicals at the end of IV. ii.

Act Four, Scene Two

Starveling is first to appear, by R door. He scratches his head, as if to say, "What *have* they been doing with my broadcloth?" Twitching a corner of the tarpaulin so as to reveal the bench underneath, he destroys in a moment the illusion of the wood, and tells us that we are in the carpenter's shop. Flute and Snout follow him from R door, and the three of them methodically fold up the tarpaulins. Quince comes last from R door.

11–14   I would give the first of these two speeches to Snout, and the scandalized correction to Quince. There is, anyway, a muddle in the speech-headings here in the Quarto, *Flute* and *Thisby* both being indicated.

15   Enter Snug, by R door.

25   Bottom is heard behind the inset curtain before he appears Centre through the curtain.

43   They carry the bench, with tarpaulins folded and trestles and tree-stump stacked on it, through the curtain. The Trap is of course closed, and the stage as bare as when the play started. Tongs-and-Bones, on a solo flute, may accompany their exit.

Act Five, Scene One

Musicians strike up with another of Morley's *Triumphs of Oriana* collection. The five-part madrigal, by George Marson, is published separately by Novello & Co., Ltd.: the words are as follows:

> The nymphs and shepherds danced
> Lavoltos in a daisy-tapstred valley.
>> Love from their face-lamps glanced,
>> Till wantonly they dally.
>> Then in a rose-banked alley
>> Bright Majesty advanced,
> A crown-graced Virgin, whom all people honour.
>> They leave their sport amazed,
>> Run all to look upon her,
>> A moment scarce they gazed
> Ere beauty's splendour all their eyes had dazed,
> Desire to see yet ever fixed on her.
>
>> Then sang the shepherds and nymphs of Diana;
>> Long live fair Oriana.

The long-drawn climax of this elaborate eulogy again serves the dramatic purpose of focussing attention on the Duke's Amazon bride.

Meanwhile there is much to do before she appears, and Philostrate must choose his moment in the music to make sure that he can get all done in time. The four attendants and the two pages, under his supervision, have to carry in, from R and L doors, a pair of heavy iron fire-dogs, about eight substantial four-foot logs, and some brush-wood. With these they build a fire over and round the Trap: they all kneel round it in a semi-circle blowing to kindle the "flames," which appear through the Trap, opened while they mask it, in the form of a red light: the effect is reinforced by smoke produced from below. At a signal from Philostrate, the attendants and pages spring away, disclosing their handiwork, and stand by for the entry of the Duke and Duchess, who come in with Egeus by R door, and go straight to warm their hands, up-stage of the fire.

That this central log-fire is as clearly a practical necessity for the staging of the play as the Couch, the Brake and the Bank of the wood setting, it would be hard to maintain. Nevertheless, something is needed for the *dead and drowsie fier* of l. 384, and for the fairies to light their tapers by, and it gives substance to Puck's line (367) *Now the wasted brands doe glowe*. Moreover, once kindled, it is very useful in giving life to the setting of the scene. Instead of the formal photographer's grouping of a conventional court-scene, we have the Elizabethan nobleman at his own fireside: the familiar lines of his first speech gain greatly from this informal setting, and when the lords and ladies sit at the front edge of the stage to watch the play, we in the audience join them in a domestic circle round the blaze (see above, pp. 34-36).

29   Lysander and Hermia, by R door. Demetrius and Helena, by L door.

42   *There is a briefe* . . . Philostrate is now acting as Master of the Revels, and has therefore supposedly witnessed all the suggested items in rehearsal: I would make this point doubly clear by having him read out the items from the brief, while Theseus comments on them. There seems to be no dramatic point in the Folio's ascription of the items to Lysander.

84   *Goe bring them in, and take your places, Ladies.* Philostrate goes to fetch the actors, through curtain, Centre. The attendants,

from R and L doors, fetch and place seats for the gentry at the
front edge of the stage. The lovers and Egeus move towards their
places, and Theseus leads Hippolyta forward to the very front of
the stage, where he makes his next speech. No one sits yet.

106 Re-enter Philostrate, through the curtain.

107 *Let him approach.* Philostrate goes back through the curtain:
     a trumpet is blown: the Court take their seats: the trumpet
sounds again: in the ensuing silent suspense, Quince puts his
head through the curtain.

125 *Who is next?* It is at this point that the inset curtain is again
     opened; and it stays open till the end of the play. The main
feature of this new setting is the foot of the great staircase, leading
up towards R inset, where the carpenter's bench is now differently
draped to make a firm landing. If a suggestion of a higher flight
of the same staircase can be made in the distance, it will add to
the beauty of the play's end. Probably the Chamberlain's Men
used the first-floor "chamber" for this purpose. Candelabra to
L of inset, at the foot of the staircase, and again half-way up, will
help the effect of palatial splendour and late-night festival: their
being extinguished at the end will make way for the different
quality of the fairies' taper-light (see above, p. 35).

126–150 The actors are disclosed by the pulling of the curtain.
         During Quince's exposition, they enact the whole story
of their play in dumb-show: the procedure is essentially the same
as in *Hamlet*, III. ii., except that there the Prologue does not
expound the dumb-show, and reserves his brief plea for a hearing
till after it.

150 Quince remains on the fore-stage, sitting on a stool as
     prompter. The rest of the actors retreat out of sight.

152 Wall advances from L inset.
The grouping for the performance of *Pyramus and Thisby* is
given in diagram on p. 132.

165 Re-enter Pyramus, R inset (that is to say, down the stairs).

185 Re-enter Thisby, L inset.

201 Pyramus goes out R inset, Thisby L inset.

203 Wall goes, L inset.
At this point the Court will clap as at the end of Scene One of
the Interlude: Theseus rises and goes up to the fire; the rest,
since the occasion is informal, may remain sitting.

208   *This is the filliest stuffe, that euer I heard.* Hippolyta's unfeeling
      comment provokes a gentle rebuke from her lover. He
turns round upon her to make his answer, and is thus facing
most of the audience when he is speaking his significant lines:
The best, in this kinde, etc. He sits again, as the play continues.

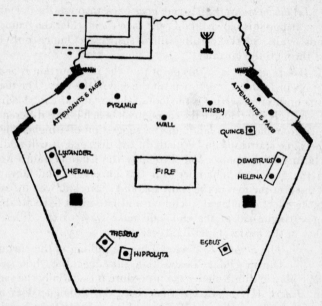

215   Re-enter Lion, L inset, and Moonshine, R inset. Moon-
      shine's dog is, I fancy, a real one. No one certainly could
read the scene of Launce's first appearance in *Two Gentlemen of
Verona* without believing that Shakespeare knew the comic effect
of the uncomprehending glance of a dog on the stage.
256   Re-enter Thisby, L inset. She runs off again by the same
      way.
262   Lion pursues her, L inset.
265   Re-enter Pyramus, R inset.
299   Exit Moonshine, R inset.
309   Re-enter Thisby, L inset.
344 ff.   The Quarto gives this speech to Lion, the Folio to
          Bottom. Dover Wilson (M.N.D., *New Cambridge Shake-
speare*, p. 149) has an interesting explanation of the different

ascription. The Folio, he says, suggests a performance without an inner-stage: its reading need not therefore concern us here. With the Quarto ascription, Lion and Moonshine bury the dead by pulling the inset-curtain: these two also dance the Bergamask. Two reasons seem to me to make this an unhappy arrangement: we do not want the curtain drawn at this point, for the Duke and Duchess and the lovers have to be seen going up the staircase to bed; secondly, Lion and Moonshine are not the obvious pair to round off the mechanicals' entertainment with a Bergamask. Can you not hear Bottom saying "Let me dance the Bergamask too"? The arrangement sketched in the following notes, though it has no support in the ascription of the printed texts, seems to me to have dramatic point and to round off the parts of the mechanicals in character.

Quince has been forgotten: he is still sitting on his stool, controlling the performance as prompter. It was he that spoke the Prologue: why should not he propose the Epilogue? Let Quince therefore speak the speech.

At the words *heare a Bergomaske daunce* . . . Bottom will struggle to his feet, and Flute with him; Bottom has planned this moment as long ago as the end of IV. i. The pair of them retire to L inset, to pick up their properties.

354   *But come your Bergomaske: let your Epilogue alone.* Bottom and
        Flute reappear from L inset: Bottom wears a paper Ass head, and Flute merely adds a paper crown to Thisby's flowing garments. The Bergamask is a very simple mime of Bottom wooing the fairy Queen, followed by an uncouth hop round the stage. The tune is, of course, the Tongs-and-Bones, on a solo flute, which Quince may if he like seem to play (see above, p. 103).

After the Bergamask, the courtiers applaud, Philostrate distributes largess, and the mechanicals are hustled off by L inset. The Duke rises and the Court with him.

362   A courtly procession up the stairs, accompanied by Mar-
        son's madrigal, probably starting from *"Then sang the shepherds and nymphs . . ."* Part at least of the procession reappears on the upper level. The attendants extinguish the candelabra, and the brilliance disappears momentarily from the scene.

At the cadence, Puck pops up through the Trap, from the dying embers.

382   *To ſweepe the duſt, behinde the dore.* A fairy, appearing from
      L inset, hands Puck a broom. Then, without music, all the
fairies come darting in from R and L doors; Oberon and Titania
last, and they stand up-stage of the glowing fire.

383–392   The fairies bear tapers. Two by two, a pair to a
          couplet, they kindle their tapers at the fire: stage-
hands in the Trap give them light. The Chamberlain's Men no
doubt were not troubled as we are with the Lord Chamberlain's
regulations for security: twentieth century fairies will hardly be
exposed to the reckless dangers of the profession in Shakespeare's
day (see above, p. 33, note 2).

393 ff.   Richmond Noble, in his *Shakespeare's Use of Song*, pp.
          55–7, discusses the music of this passage, and makes it
plain that the Song begins with two lines of solo for Oberon, the
fairies joining in at *To the beſt bride bed will wee* . . . and ending at
. . . *Shall vpon their children be.*

It is unlikely—indeed, I think, impossible—that one could
find an existing piece of contemporary music to fit the intricate
rhythm of these lines. Something must be invented for the
occasion. For completeness, and in case other producers may
care to adopt it, Hector McCurrach's setting of the words is here
given. If Oberon is not a singer, he may be allowed to speak his
lines.

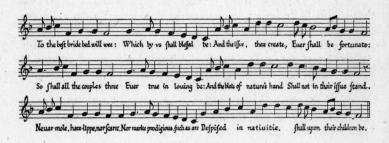

To the beſt bride bed will wee: Which by vs ſhall bleſſel   be: And the iſſue , that create, Euer ſhall be fortunate:

So ſhall all the couples three Euer   true in louing be: And the blots of nature's hand Shall not in their iſſue ſtand.

Neuer mole, hare-lippe, nor ſcarre, Nor marke prodigious, ſuch as are Deſpiſed   in natiuitie,   ſhall vpon their children be.

During the twelve lines of the Song, the fairies perform a ritual
purification of the great hall represented by the stage and the
theatre, lifting their tapers aloft to give solemnity to their rite.
Throughout, they seem to be singing the Song together with their
invisible reinforcements, aloft in the gallery.

411–414 These four lines dove-tailed thus into the Weelkes
ballet *On the plains:*

Trippe away: make no ſtay is thus made to echo the rhythm of the
opening phrase.

While the rest of the ballet is being sung, Puck holds a leafy
cup of field-dew, into which each fairy dips a hand and trips up
the stair. Half go before, half after Oberon and Titania, who
pause for a moment on the upper level: as the music comes to a
full close, Puck springs forward, while the inset-curtain is pulled
to behind his back; then he plunges into the Trap. This is the
true end of the play.

415–430 Puck climbs out of the Trap again, to speak the
Epilogue, which is a mere graceful formality.

The following are the published madrigals and part-songs used in the Elizabethan score suggested in the appendix.

All creatures now are merry, merry-minded   John Bennet
    (from Morley's *The Triumphs of Oriana*, 1601)

On the plains, Fairy trains   Thomas Weelkes
    (1598)

Lullaby, my sweet little Baby   William Byrd
    (from *Psalms, Sonnets and Songs*, 1588)

Draw on, sweet Night   John Wilbye
    (1609)

The nymphs and shepherds danced   George Marson
    (from Morley's *The Triumphs of Oriana*, 1601)

(The first four are published by Messrs. Stainer & Bell, Ltd., and Marson's madrigal by Messrs. Novello & Co., Ltd.)